Royal Tunbridge Wells

A History

Hungershall Park, facing Nevill Park across the fields.

Royal Tunbridge Wells

A History

C.W. Chalklin

Phillimore

2008

Published by
PHILLIMORE & CO. LTD
Chichester, West Sussex, England
www.phillimore.co.uk
www.thehistorypress.co.uk

ISBN 978-1-86077-526-0

Printed and bound in Great Britain

Contents

Part Two: The Growth of the Modern Town

List of Illustrations

Acknowledgements

Part One was begun many years ago based on research by the author; it has been revised to include material from more recent histories. For Part Two the author is indebted in particular to C.H. Strange 'The History of Tunbridge Wells' in J.C.M. Given (ed.), *Royal Tunbridge Wells Past and Present for the Occasion of the Jubilee Congress of the South-Eastern Union of Scientific Societies July 1946* (Tunbridge Wells, 1946), to Alan Savidge, *Royal Tunbridge Wells* (Speldhurst, 1975), an attractive history in which the visitors and the public buildings and churches are amply described, to Roger Farthing, *A History of Mount Sion, Tunbridge Wells* (Chichester, 2003), a hugely detailed study, and the useful publications of the Local History Group of the Royal Tunbridge Wells Civic Society. It also includes much original material, especially from local directories published since the 1860s.

The author's wife, Mavis, and daughter, Heather Morgan, helped indispensably in photographing buildings in Tunbridge Wells. The production team at Phillimore advised on and handled the processing of the manuscript and pictures efficiently. The British Library kindly permitted the reproduction of four photographs in its custody, as detailed in the sources. The Tunbridge Wells Reference Library allowed the author to study its comprehensive collection of books and pamphlets. Material in the Kent Archaeological Society Library, Maidstone Museum, and the Tonbridge Reference Library was also used.

Introduction

Spa towns form a distinct type of town. Royal Tunbridge Wells is no exception. There are two aspects to the history of such towns. On the one hand there is the society of the visitors and leisured residents, their daily habits, their intercourse and their entertainments. These are described in contemporary guide books, diaries, letters and novels, and have since become a familiar chapter in English social history. In particular the life of the visitors at Tunbridge Wells was described by L. Melville in *Society at Tunbridge Wells* (1912), R.V. Lennard in *Englishmen at Rest and Play* (1931), Margaret Barton, *A History of Tunbridge Wells* (1937), and more recently by A. Savidge in *Royal Tunbridge Wells*, and other writers. On the the other hand the planning and building of the town, the owners of the houses and amenities, the professional, trades and craftsmen were largely ignored until quite recently. The author began the study of the creation of the town between 1680 and 1840 in the 1960s, and has been followed by Savidge, Roger Farthing in *A History of Mount Sion: Tunbridge Wells* (2003), and a series of recent publications by the Tunbridge Wells Civic Society. This book is a survey of the history of the local community. While drawing on all these works, it includes much new material.

The site of Tunbridge Wells was a wilderness of forest and heath where the Kentish parishes of Speldhurst and Tonbridge met the Sussex parish of Frant. It is likely that the medicinal value of its waters were known locally in Elizabethan times. Within a few years of their discovery by London society in 1606, the Wells had become one of the leading English watering places. In the 1680s and '90s, when its permanent popularity as a resort was assured, there was a building boom in which the capital and enterprise of London speculators teamed with the efforts of local builders to create the celebrated Pantiles and hills covered with lodging houses. A new community of perhaps about 1,000 people with its chapels and school came into being, depending for its livelihood on the exploitation of the summer visitors. The 18th century was a period of slower development. Towards its end a leisured class of retired professional and business men, and single gentlewomen began to settle at the Wells. After 1800 their number grew large, and by 1841 the population had increased sevenfold. With the building of housing estates and churches, and the grant of self-governing powers to the town in 1835, this period saw the beginning of modern Tunbridge Wells.

The town continued to grow; it was reached by the railway in 1846, became a borough in 1889 and was designated 'Royal' in 1909. While it had a modest role as a trading centre for north-east Sussex, its livelihood was still mainly based on more and more visitors and prosperous residents. Light manufacturing was almost negligible in size, though the town was famous for the making of Tunbridge Ware. The wealth of the town was seen in the large number of big houses, in spacious gardens often adjoining the Common and parks, and in its churches and a variety of public buildings including the Grand Hall and the Opera House. The population was stationary between 1911 and 1931, being 35,568 and 35,367 in those two years. The summer visitors remained important until the 1950s and 1960s, there was still a leisured population and the number of commuters to London grew steadily from the 1920s. Accompanying the emergence of a small industrial estate, the town grew as a commercial centre in East Sussex and in some respects as an administrative centre for south-east England. The retired inhabitants and the commuters also explain the rise in population from 38,397 in 1951 to 44,506 in 1971. The general reorganisation of local government of 1974 led to the creation of a much enlarged Borough of Royal Tunbridge Wells.

Part One:
The Rise of the Spa Town, 1680-1835

I The Emergence of the Town

The Early Spa

At the beginning of the 17th century the cult of the watering place as a health resort was growing. 'The use of springs for therapeutic bathing, and the drinking of medicinal waters, had become firmly established forms of treatment in England before the Civil War. Already medical men were earnestly discussing the best means of using these natural remedies.' The best season, the length of treatment, the diet and exercise which should accompany the cure, and the illnesses for which the springs were efficacious were all being eagerly debated.[1] Soon people were flocking to the spas for whom bathing and drinking for health reasons were only a pretext; the resorts were becoming centres of entertainment and diversion for fashionable society. The hundred years after the Restoration was the golden age of the English spa. Seabathing was still regarded with disfavour, continental travel was difficult and often dangerous, and the wild beauty of the mountain regions of the British Isles as yet unappreciated.

Some of the springs had been known for centuries, such as those at Bath, while others, like those at Harrogate, found in 1570, or at Epsom, in 1618, were discoveries. A reference on an Elizabethan local map to 'Welspryngate' suggests that the iron-impregnated waters on the site of Tunbridge Wells were known in the district to be of medicinal value. In 1606 London society was told of their value by Dudley, Lord North, after his visit to Lord Bergavenny at Eridge in Frant. As London physicians confirmed their healing potentialities, the popularity of the waters was almost immediate. In 1619 John Chamberlain could write that 'the waters at Tunbridge … for these three or fowre years have been much frequented, especially this sommer by many great persons'. Bergavenny (died 1622) had wells dug over two of the springs, the site cleared and paved, and the road to it improved. Although the site lay in Speldhurst parish, it became known as Tunbridge Wells because Tonbridge was the nearest town. When in 1629 Queen Henrietta Maria visited the Wells (where she slept in a tent) to recuperate after the birth of her first child, fashionable approval was given to it; only 35 miles from London, it offered a pleasant change from the summer heat of the capital. In 1632 Lodowick Rowzee, a doctor with knowledge of continental spas, wrote *The Queenes Wells, or the Nature and Virtue of Tunbridge Water*. Peers, ladies, knights and London merchants were there every year. It was said that in 1636 a shelter was provided for the ladies and another for the gentlemen, and two years later a long green bank was made and levelled and planted with a double row of trees to form an avenue for the company to walk along after drinking at the wells. Lodgings, much in demand during the season, were found in the few manor houses, farmhouses and cottages in the hamlets of Rusthall over a mile to the west, and Southborough two miles to the north, and even in Tonbridge five miles away; by 1639 tenements were being erected for lodgings in the hamlets. The Wells continued to be visited in the 1640s and 1650s for medical reasons; in some years from 1648 during the aftermath of the Civil Wars and the Interregnum, the Council of State feared that the district was the centre of royalist or dissident plots.[2]

After the Restoration as the number attending for diversion began to exceed those coming for health reasons, it grew yet more popular. Visits were encouraged by the patronage of royalty. Charles II, his Queen and the Duke of York were there several times from 1660 to 1674. By then the Wells ranked second only to Bath as a health resort, and may have equalled it as a fashionable rendezvous on account of being much nearer London. Ministers and government officials were able to handle public business by letter while they enjoyed the entertainments and country air.[3]

The history of the settlement began about 70 years later than that of the spa. Up to 1680 it was a barren spot and the nearest hamlet was over a mile distant. A road from Tonbridge town through Southborough to Frant ran near the wells, which lay in a valley at the bottom of a common of 249 acres, then called Bishops Down, belonging to the manor of Rusthall. The surrounding hills were wooded and heathland. In 1664 Lord Muskerry of Somerhill mansion near Tonbridge, lord of the manor by right of his wife, had built a stone wall with an elaborate gateway and with a basin over the main spring. There was now a hall to shelter the water dippers. In the 1670s a few illicit tenements, taverns and shops were erected on the waste which was part of the Common alongside the avenue, now becoming known as the Upper Walk after a Lower Walk was made beside it. According to a contemporary, tradesmen exposed their wares on stalls and musicians entertained the company under the trees as late as 1680, while no one stopped cattle wandering over the

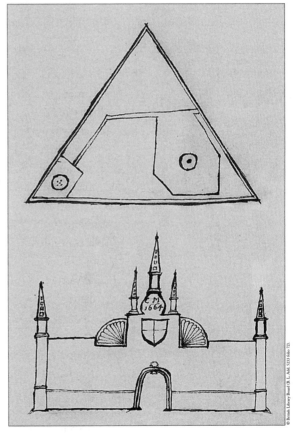

1 *The triangular site of the main well as paved by Lord Charles Muskerry in 1664, with the wall and gateway surmounted by his initials, the date and his coat of arms.*

Walks. Apart from drinking the waters, the company talked as they walked up and down the Upper Walk or gambled with dice or cards or kettlepins or, after 1678, attended the adjoining chapel on a nearby site given by Viscountess Purbeck of Somerhill.

No lodging houses had yet been built on the neighbouring hills. In Rawlins' *Tunbridge Wells, or a Days Courtship: a Comedy* of 1678 some of the characters stayed at Rusthall and Southborough, where another writer suggested they danced or played bowls, already a fashionable pastime in the 17th century; other visitors lodged with the neighbouring gentry, like the 'gentleman of the town' in the play, who resided at Bounds, a mansion near Southborough, 'with several wealthy heirs under the same roof'; Somerhill also lodged some of the company. When the Court came in the 1660s most slept in tents, although no one in the play did so too.[4]

The delay in building houses near the Wells was mainly due to the desolate nature of the site. As early as 1572 the spa of Buxton had 'a very goodly house … and other goodly lodgings to the number of thirty' for those coming to its waters, built by a wealthy patron, but there would seem to have been at least a village there before. By 1628 Bath was highly organised and well-equipped to meet the needs of visitors, being 'beautified with fair and goodly buildings for the receipt of strangers'; yet it had always been a town. As Tunbridge Wells was not even a hamlet it was natural that lodgings should be found first in existing dwellings, and that new accommodation should be built nearby. Only when the permanent popularity of the spa was assured were people

2   A fanciful picture of visitors at the well in 1678.

ready to build lodging houses and shops on a new site solely for the benefit of summer visitors.[5]

Yet when at last building began, the town grew rapidly. In 1680 the first lodging houses were erected in Culverden Woods, on the north-west side of the Common. Two years later rows of shops began to appear on the Walks near the wells. Finally, from 1685, lodging houses were built on the hill, to be known as Mount Sion, a few hundred yards to the east of the Walks, and further north near the Common. The 1680s and 1690s saw a building boom which was not to be repeated until the construction of the Calverley Estate in the years from 1829. It's importance is shown by the Turnpike Act of 1709 to improve the last 10 miles of the road from London to the Wells (8 Anne c.20).

The Building of the Shops

Although the isolation of the site was the chief reason for the delay in the growth of a settlement, another factor helped to slow the appearance of buildings on the waste by the Walks near the wells. Many of the freeholders of Rusthall Manor let lodgings at Rusthall or Southborough. They naturally feared the competition of lodging houses so near to the wells, and as they held common rights on the waste their consent was necessary if the land was to be leased for building. The court of the manor ordered the removal of several booths erected without permission, and about 1680 one building erected by a mercer, Richard Constable, was demolished by the freeholders. This was despite the fact that Constable had rented the manor from Lady Purbeck. Finally the manor was bought from Viscountess Purbeck by Thomas Neale, a London businessman and speculator. He persuaded some of the freeholders to let him lease the land by agreeing that the buildings should only be shops and not lodging houses. By a lease of 30 August 1682 from Neale and some of the freeholders to Thomas Janson, who was Neale's agent, the Walks and the adjoining land within 12 yards passed to Janson for 50 years. This was the normal London term for a building lease. The tenants were compensated for their loss of common rights in the land by a rent of 10s. a year each. The most important clause was that Janson might erect 'any gallery, shop, booth, shed, coffee room, drinking room and playing room for the conveniency, accommodation, pastime and divertisement of the gentry who so come to drink the waters, so long as it is not a dwelling house, lodging rooms or chimneys for dressing meat'. Janson was also to maintain the Walks and see that they were kept clear of building.[6]

Plots for building were laid out in two rows adjoining the Walks, running south-westwards for about 175 yards from the wells.

Leases by the lord began just over two years after his agreement with the freeholders. The first lease was to Thomas Weller, a lawyer in Tonbridge town, on 5 December 1684. The parcel lay between the Upper Walk and the unenclosed Common, having a frontage of 40 feet and depth of 28 feet. The building to be erected had to be roofed with slate or tile, that is, not thatch, and not raised so high as to prejudice the air of the Walks. The right to make a sewer from a cellar under the Walks to the sewer recently dug on the other side was allowed if the ground was levelled afterwards. These covenants suggest that the lord and the freeholders wished to ensure that the rustic charm of the Walks was not damaged by the new building. They were trying to prevent at the Wells the nuisances with which nearly every town of the time was inflicted, and which might well have driven away the company.[7]

Weller's lease was for 41 years at £4 per annum. Twelve leases were granted in the next three years on similar terms. No more were made until 1691, and the leases of the 1690s were not of building plots, but of houses already erected. Most were conveyances to their builders, and may either have been erected illicitly or by prior agreement during the previous decade.

Contemporaries were unanimous about the transformation which followed the lease of 1682. In a lawsuit 50 years later between the lord and the freeholders, John Archer, a cordwainer, said that before 1682 the only tenements had been a barber's shop built of timber and roofed with tiles, three or four butchers' shops built of alderpoles, daubed with loam and roofed with thatch, and

3 *Tunbridge Wells Common, part of the waste of the manor of Rusthall on which building was prohibited.*

Constable's shop with a chamber over it where his servant used to sleep; after the Janson lease many tenements were erected within three or four years. Another witness, John Fuggle, who had been apprenticed in London in 1678, found on his return eight years later several shops standing in a row from Constable's shop at the far end of the Walks up to the wells. He described them as 'flatt shops', with only garrets above for the shopkeepers. In obedience to the covenant in the lease of 1682 none had chambers above them to lodge visitors. Fuggle, who was employed by his wife's uncle as a joiner in finishing his house on the Walks, remembered his wife carrying the food for cooking to her neighbour who lived outside the bounds of the manor. Several houses were pulled down by the freeholders as they were being built because they contained kitchens and lodging rooms.

In June 1688, however, many of the wooden buildings were burnt down, affecting 11 households, and the freeholders were less successful afterwards in keeping the new tenements within the terms of the 1682 lease. Some buildings were erected as lodging houses and some as shops; probably one or two floors were added to the older booths. At the manorial court in 1694 seven people were fined for letting lodgings, 'dressing meat', or building chimneys on the Walks. Yet most of the buildings were still partly shops, for when the traveller Celia Fiennes visited the Wells in 1697 she found 'a row of buildings ... which are all shops'.[8]

Probably the great phase of building was now complete, 15 years after the 1682 lease. The row of buildings on the north-west side of the Walks mentioned by Fiennes included 'two large coffee houses for tea, chocolate etc.', coffee houses being meeting rooms for merchants and brokers in London, 'and two rooms for the lottery and hazard board; these are all built with an arch or penthouse beyond the shops some of which are supported by pillars like a peesa [piazza; in this sense a colonnade in front of buildings] which is paved with brick and stone for the dry walking of the company in rain'. Thus the buildings were already contiguous. The pavement was laid with pantiles in 1700. The evidence of six shops 20 years later suggests that they were partly timber and partly brick. A rental of about 1700 mentioned perhaps 20 or 25 shops in the row, including 'three wood shops' selling woodwork, a barber, a watchmaker and an 'Indian gownman'. Opposite there was a short middle row of three or four little booths. On the other side the Lower Walk contained part of the market for which the right was obtained by Lord Bergavenny in 1686, by 1719 it was called the Fish Market to distinguish it from the market site in front of the wells, and at the end adjoining the wells there were up to 20 more shops. They included two barbers, an apothecary, an upholsterer and a chandler, with the Gloucester Tavern, as named after the boy Duke of Gloucester who visited the Wells with his mother Princess Anne, a coffee house and 'pissing house'. In 1719 the Gloucester had three storeys with garrets, and the shop on the wells side of the market had two storeys and garrets.[9]

The agreement between the lord and the freeholders soon led to disputes. There were three points of dissension which were not settled until 1739: firstly, not all the freeholders had agreed to the lease; secondly the covenant against the building of lodging houses was not properly enforced; and thirdly no provision had been made for the disposal of the properties at the end of the 50-year term.

The first problem came to a head in 1711. Two freeholders, Richard Mercer and William Camfield, who had not signed but refused the original lease, pulled down a shop on the Walks erected by Wood, a lessee of the lord. The latter brought an action of trespass, and the case was tried at Maidstone. A verdict was given that the freeholders who had not joined in the lease of 1682 were to execute a lease from 30 August 1711, to expire at the same time.

After 1700 the rooms for lodgings grew steadily as shops were converted or had rooms added on top. In a chancery suit of 1729 Mathew Wesley, a local apothecary, said that one Michael Elmes had built a house and shop on the Walks about 33 or 34 years earlier; he himself had held it for 13 years before 1720 and had let rooms to lodgers and dressed meat; and only last summer his sister and niece had stayed there and cooked food. About 1714 James Latter, a turner, had been the tenant of two shops on the Walks, and had filled several rooms with lodgers. When the freeholders threatened to sue him for breach of covenant he stopped having lodgers, except occasionally by stealth. By the 1720s what the freeholders had feared would happen nearly 50 years earlier, was becoming a reality: their lodging houses at Rusthall and Southborough were becoming increasingly deserted in favour of, not only the houses on the hills, but also of the rooms on the Walks. Yet from the point of view of the lord and his tenants on the Walks, their properties would have been halved in value if the covenants against lodgings had been enforced.[10]

After 1732, when the 50-year lease to the lord expired, this problem became overshadowed by the dispute about the ownership of the Walks and the buildings. The lord claimed that they were on land that had been part of the demesne of the manor, and so in his outright ownership, and thus the buildings were his own property. In reply the freeholders stressed that the lease of 1682 showed that the land had been waste; the houses interfered with their rights of common, and they threatened to demolish them and lay open the Walks for their cattle. In this conflict they were led by the Earl of Abergavenny (formerly Bergavenny), a freeholder and a large landowner in Frant parish, and himself the owner of a row of houses on the south-east side of the Walks, near the county boundary, which had been built by 1719, presumably on building lease. Probably he was jealous that the Walks and the wells lay in Rusthall Manor and not on his own land. The lord accused him of

4 *Tunbridge Wells in 1719.*

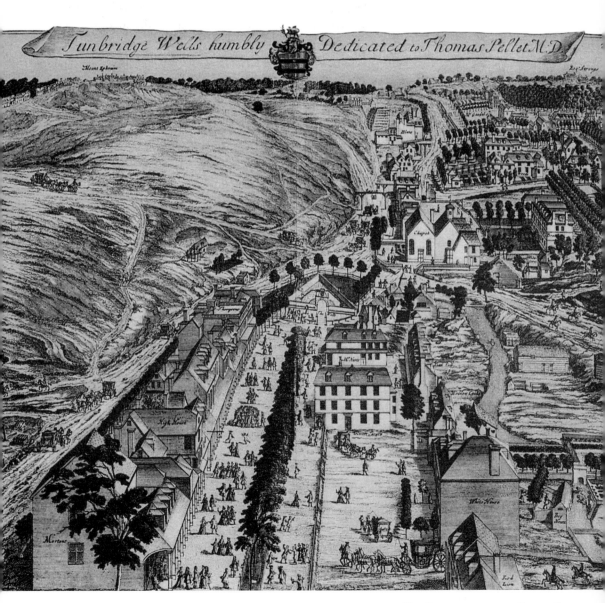

wanting to take advantage of the confusion to enclose the Walks within his own estate. At least he wished to cut down some of the trees and rails beside the Lower Walk to allow access from his own lodging houses and taverns. Naturally he helped to finance the costly suits in law and equity that the freeholders undertook against the lord of the manor and his tenants between 1732 and 1739.

A settlement was finally reached in 1739, confirmed by an Act of Parliament. The buildings on the Walks were divided into three lots: two became the share of the lord, and the third was assigned to the freeholders. This last was to be held in trust, the profits being divided among the freeholders in proportion to the value of their properties held by the manor. Further building was carefully restricted: only in one place could new houses or shops be erected, and no other part of the waste of the manor was to be built on without the mutual consent of the lord and freeholders. These rules ensured that the original plan of the buildings, consisting of two rows of houses, was not disturbed.

5 *The Common, showing a house which escaped demolition under the rule that the waste was not to be built on; before 1739 there were complaints of new roads and tracks damaging the Common.*

Covenants similar to those in the original building leases were added to the agreement: no sewers were to be dug within 30 feet of the wells; no 'necessary house' was to be erected on any part of the premises; and no cellar or vault was to be dug more than seven feet below the level of the pavement. Thus again special care was taken to prevent the nuisances which damaged nearly every town of the time and to protect the drinking waters. The covenants were essential if the Walks were to stay the centre of the fashionable life of the spa. Finally Lord Abergavenny was allowed to build a covered walk from his houses to the Upper Walk.[11]

After the end of the great phase of building on the Walks before about 1700, it is likely that only a few houses were erected in the next 40 years, though several of the existing tenements were extended or rebuilt. A map of 1738 made at the time of the agreement shows every building and its dimensions. There were 25 tenements in the main row of shops on the north-west side of the Walks. The largest were probably public rooms: the Great

Room had a frontage of 82 feet and the Long Room of 54 feet; the smallest tenements were four buildings with a total frontage of 56 feet, similar to that of four typical town houses. Their depth varied between 47 and 11 feet. The larger houses backed onto the Common and the smaller onto similar buildings facing the Common. Except for three alleys they were contiguous, with the covered walk beside the shop fronts.

The main or Upper Walk, the chief place of promenade for the company, was about 30 feet broad and paved with pantiles, from which the name of the Walks derives. On the south-east side was a row of trees, interspersed by four small huts. Two were of two tenements, the largest single one measuring only 14 by nine feet. The Lower Walk, 'chiefly used by country people and servants' lay on the other side of the trees. At the far end it was in its turn bounded by trees on the south-eastern side. Half way towards the wells was the Gloucester Tavern and an adjoining tenement. Then came the open Fish Market, so called because fish from Rye and Hastings was a major commodity. Finally, nearer the wells, there was a row of probably 13 humbler shops, about 200-feet long. These were much smaller than the buildings on the Upper

6 *The Pantiles in 1748; a well-known picture of celebrated people standing on the Upper Walk with the colonnade on the left.*

Walk; most had frontages of under 20 feet, and two were mere booths nine-feet long. There were several buildings behind the row, including a stable, 'hog court' for pigs, and 'pissing houses'.[12] The buildings were of one storey with garrets, or of two storeys. By now many occupiers let their upper rooms to visitors, and the ground floors were shops with a few taverns and public rooms. The annual value of the estate in 1739 was £1,123 1s. Although the buildings had hardly increased, it was almost three times the rental 40 years earlier. As the long building leases had expired in the 1720s the lord had re-leased the properties for shorter terms at much higher rents. Thus William Vandernan had a lease of the Great Room on the Upper Walk at £188 annually for 11 years; and seven other properties paid over £50. On the other hand the smaller buildings in the lower row paid £10 or less.[13]

Little evidence has been traced about the row of buildings on the Abergavenny Estate. One assumes that they were also erected by building leases during the boom of the 1680s and 90s. Kip's engraving (1718 or 1719) shows the ground opposite the Pantiles fully occupied by three or four short rows of one- or two-storey buildings all with garrets, one of which was called

the Red Lion. In between was a large three-storey building with garrets called the White House. They were identified in 1738 on the first map as taverns and lodging houses. The White House was now Morleys Coffee House facing the Pantiles with Todds Great Rooms attached behind. Scattered in the rear were the Sussex Tavern, its stables and brewhouse. They stayed in this form; much later in 1766 T.B. Burr wrote that they all comprised a few decent lodging houses, taverns, and an elegant assembly room with a coffee house.[14]

The Building of the Lodging Houses

As the Walks contained the wells, parades, shops and the market it was the centre of the pleasure and commerce of the growing settlement. Yet at the same time as the shops were being erected, lodging houses were appearing in two different places at a distance from the Walks. One site, known as Mount Ephraim, lay in the Culverden Woods, along the north-west edge of the Common, and near the road from Southborough and Tonbridge to the Wells. It was a commanding position, looking down across

LEASES AND BUILDING ON THE BICKERSTAFFE ESTATE BY NOVEMBER 1684

Date of Lease	Acreage	Term	Rent	Lessee	Assignee	The Buildings
1 Jan 1680	4 acres, Upper Culverden	50 years	£1	John Fulman of Tonbridge, sawyer	Sir Thomas Janson of St Martin in the Fields, Westminster, baronet	built on by Fulman, then assigned 'for a considerable sum'
27 May 1682	6 acres, Lower Culverden	50 years	£2 10s.	Richard Dorsett of Rusthall, butcher	Sit Thomas Janson	built on by Dorsett, Janson spent £1,500 on additional houses
10 Jan 1683	23 acres, Lower Culverden; Curds Coppice (18 acres); 4 acres, Upper Culverden	47 years	£15 10s.	John Skynner, girdler, of the City	None	erected 'several great buildings'; sublet land and tenants also built; total outlay £5,000
3 Sep 1683	8 acres, Upper Culverden	47 Years	£4	John, Richard and Samuel Waggon of Pembury, bricklayers	None	spent £500 on building
8 Nov 1683	Upper Culverden	46 years	£2	Abraham Spooner, vintner, of the City	None	spent £1,200 on building

the Common to the Walks half a mile below. Finding it 'very convenient on which to erect buildings for the entertainment of such visitors as yearly resort to the Wells', several people leased land for building from the owner, Sir Charles Bickerstaffe of Wilderness, near Sevenoaks, between 1679 and 1683. The one surviving building lease, to Samuel Cooke of Speldhurst, a pailmaker, on 1 January 1680 with the condition that at least £100 was spent on a 'substantial new messuage' suggests that a dwelling large enough for a lodging house was intended. The earliest lease was probably that to Richard Constable, the local mercer, in September 1679. Details have survived in a chancery lawsuit about building on five other plots. The land was let on the same long terms as on the Walks at a ground rent, in parcels large enough for several houses with meadow or pasture attached. There was immediate building on a large scale. After the first two or three years London merchants spent huge sums to supplement the more modest outlay of local men. Skynner and his tenants spent £5,000, the three Pembury bricklayers £500. After the building of the first lodging houses an assembly room, a house with two banqueting rooms, a bowling green and at least one tavern followed. The estate was mortgaged in the early 1680s, and at least one parcel was sold as early as 1687.[15]

Building declined after the 1680s on account of the development of another site much closer to the Walks. Surviving title deeds from the early 18th century do not mention new houses. Stagnation is suggested by a reference in 1737 to a 'toft on which a messuage lately stood, now taken down', and in 1755 to an 'old decayed messuage called the Fish Pond House', a place of amusement. Burr in 1766 confirmed and explained the arrested development: owing to its distance from the Pantiles the place 'has lost much of its former regard'; the assembly room had gone, the bowling green was now 'a common field', and the taverns had become private houses. Yet because of its fine air and position it was still a respectable quarter for lodgings, away from the showy amusements of the public place.[16]

The map of 1738 shows the building which spread unevenly along the edge of the Common for about half a mile. There were about 30 or 40 buildings, most were houses with a few barns, stables and other outbuildings. Some had just yards and gardens, like the 'messuage' or tenement with stables, workshop, buildings, yard and garden occupied by William Mercer in 1737. The land behind was free of buildings, although attached to some of the houses, and mostly converted from woodland into meadow or pasture to make small farm holdings.

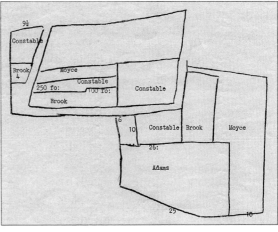

7 *Plan of part of the building land on Mount Sion, 1686.*

The building site of Mount Sion was about 16 acres on a sharp slope above the Common a few hundred yards from the Walks. A little building also occurred on another short hill to the north called Mount Pleasant, and for about half a mile northwards near the Common and the road from Southborough to where the Common joined Culverden. The estate was a heath called Inhams extending to Calverley Plain, all owned by Viscountess Purbeck as lady of the manor of Southfrith. As at Culverden, no common rights existed. With her steward, Thomas Weller, the Viscountess made the first building lease at the end of 1684, five years after the first lease on Mount Ephraim. Obviously the immediate success of the Bickerstaffe development encouraged this new extensive scheme.

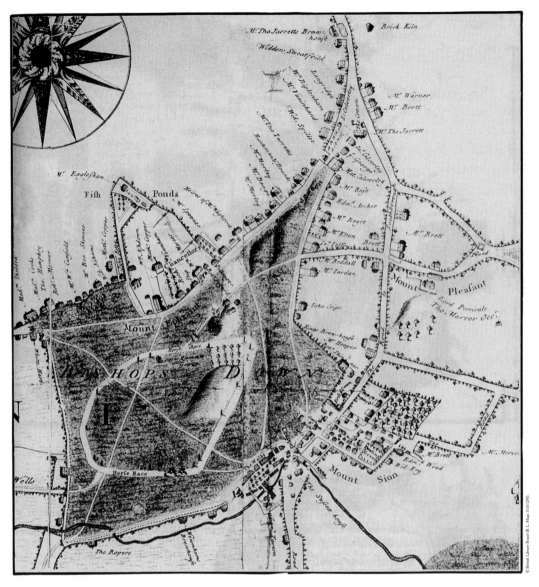

Map of Tunbridge Wells in 1738 by John Bowra; it is the first surviving general plan.

8 *Map of Tunbridge Wells in 1738 by John Bowra; it is the first surviving general plan.*

According to Farthing, between 1684 and 1696 Viscountess Purbeck made 33 leases almost always for 50 years. A few of the tenants including Richard Constable and a Speldhurst wheelwright, Edward White, took more than one lease. The first nine leases were dated 4 November 1684, and about one third were completed in that month; a third more were made by October 1687. The total area was probably about 200 acres and the ground rents worth £189 17s. 6d. The value of the land depended on its distance from the Walks. While a 12-acre part of Calverley Plain was let to Richard Constable on 20 May 1687 for £5, a four-acre part of Calverley Plain near the Walks was let at Michaelmas 1687 to a barber named Edmund Reeves for £6. Smaller plots near the

Walks and the road near the Common were let as sites for lodging houses and a greater acreage more distant was converted for grazing. Some of the Mount Sion plots formed strips stretching uphill. The development was thus carefully planned.[17]

It was an indication of the demand for building land that the plots were divided and sub-leased almost immediately. From the parcel totaling over 22 acres leased to Robert Brook and Richard Constable in November 1684 for £7, a piece three rods 10 feet by four rods two feet, another 40 rods by 10 rods, and a third three

9 *Plan of Mount Sion in 1738 by Bowra.*

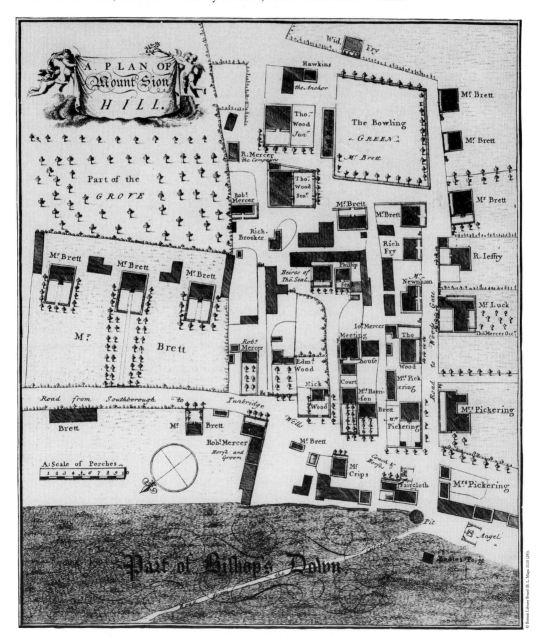

rods by three and a half rods, were demised (possibly with other land) to Thomas Moyce, of Tonbridge parish, a yeoman, for £3. He in turn on 20 September 1687 leased these little parcels to Philip Seale, a Tonbridge glazier for 47 years at £1 annually. Four and a half years later Seale acquired a further parcel from Edward Martin, a joiner also of Tonbridge, for 42 years 11 months at £1 5s. a year. The sub-leases were to expire on the same date as all the principal leases. Presumably in many cases the original lessee built one or two houses, possibly to the limit of his capital or what he was able to borrow on mortgage, and then sub-leased part of the remaining land at a higher rent. Both Edward Martin and Thomas Moyce had their own houses and sub-leased land.[18]

10 *One of the earliest houses on Mount Ephraim, presumably built in the 1680s or 1690s.*

As on Mount Ephraim building began as soon as, or soon after, the leases were granted. The new lodging houses were accompanied by a bowling green by 1692. Farthing estimated that 53 houses were built on the Southfrith land between 1684 and 1699. In 1707, and probably several years earlier, there were houses near the Common and the Pantiles, and on both sides of the road from Southborough. As shown on the map, by 1738 the buildings on Mount Sion formed a rough square, including the Grove at the north-east corner, whilst a few lay between the Common and the road, and the rest on the hillside to the east. These buildings were detached and many were surrounded by trees. All had courts, backyards and gardens, and most had coach houses, barns and stables. The bowling green had a ballroom attached. Apart from at least three taverns, they were lodging and dwelling houses. There were about a dozen houses along the edge of the Common northwards to Culverden, where there were two taverns, the Crown and the George, a brewhouse, shop and several cottages. Presumably because the builders were mainly local, the size of their investments of perhaps £200 or £300 involved just one or two lodging houses.

Like the Culverden Estate, by the end of the 17th century the Southfrith demesne had become heavily mortgaged owing to the financial embarrassment of its owners. Most of the buildings were sold by the Earl of Buckingham between 1702 and 1710, sometimes to the lessee. In 1702 Thomas Weller bought the tenements on his leasehold land at Culverden, and Philip Seale bought his leasehold property on Mount Sion. Originally the town was built on the three estates of Culverden, Southfrith and Eridge, and the parcel of the waste leased to the Rusthall lord of the manor. Now with the partition and sale of two of these properties, over half the buildings of the new town were small freeholds; many were occupied by their new owners.

Altogether in 1738 there were about 100 or 120 houses on Mount Ephraim, Mount Sion and the land between, apart from the shops and lodging houses on the Pantiles. Most had been built by 1700 and nearly all by 1710. They were timber-framed and hung with tiles; the earliest brick house on Mount Sion was built sometime between 1710 and 1738. The boom of the 1680s and '90s was the result of the previous delay and then the release of the pent-up demand as land for building suddenly became available, and Thomas Neale and other Londoners invested large sums. One must assume that by the 1700s demand was roughly satisfied and did not grow much until the 1720s and 1730s. Too many lodging houses may have been built by the end of the 1690s, though overbuilding was only temporary. Possibly Princess Anne's decision not to visit the Wells after 1699 influenced other visitors. However, the partial fall in the attraction of Mount Ephraim in the early 18th century was probably caused by the increase in lodging houses on the Pantiles and the continued popularity of Mount Sion.[19]

The general view of these scattered houses, interspersed with trees, must have been striking. Equally pleasant were closer pictures of the Pantiles, with the colonnade running the whole length of the Upper Walk and the row of trees on the other side, or of Mount Sion, with its houses set amongst trees. The names Mounts Ephraim and Sion may reflect Puritan visits to the Wells during the aftermath of the Civil Wars.

11 *Jerningham House, built on a lease of 1689 by Edward Allen, presumably as a lodging house.*

In a smaller way, Southborough had a similar history to Mount Ephraim as a site of lodgings. For a time after 1680 the lodging houses nearer the Pantiles did not interfere with the prosperity of Southborough. In fact it shared in the building boom, presumably because it lay by the road to the Wells. Where the Southfrith demesne reached the hamlet, Lady Purbeck leased 50 acres for 50 years to William Kitchenham of Tonbridge on 8 November 1684, within a few days of the earliest Mount Sion lease. He built 'two fair houses' with barns, stables and coachhouses to combine lodging houses with a small farm, and a year later he sub-leased 12 acres to a Rotherfield 'gentleman' for 48

12 *Two Mount Sion lodging houses built in 1689 and 1694 by Philip Seale, a glazier.*

years, and Fermor in his turn built a 'fair house and a coachhouse'. Small owner-occupiers built houses and shops on their land.[20]

Development probably slowed at the same time as that at the Wells. By the 1720s the lodging houses both at Southborough and at Rusthall were feeling the full effect of the competition of the houses at the Wells with many falling into disuse. In 1734 John Archer of Speldhurst, a cordwainer, said that for several years some had been empty, and had either been pulled down or used by cottagers, 'inhabited only by poor labouring men at very low rents'. Even Great Bounds, the home of Sydney Stafford Smythe, Esquire, which had formerly lodged Princess Anne and all the best company, had had no visitors for a few years.[21] Whereas before the 1680s all the visitors had lodged at least a mile or two from the Wells, by 1740 nearly everyone stayed within half a mile.

The Builders

If any one family can be termed the patrons of the Wells in its earliest years, it is that of the owners of the manor of Southfrith living at Somerhill: Lord Muskerry (died 1664), his wife Viscountess Purbeck (died 1698), and her son the *soi-disant* Earl of Buckingham. After the Restoration Lord Muskerry, as lord of the manor of Rusthall, developed the facilities for drinking the waters and improved the Walks. Although his wife later sold the manor, these changes helped to make the Pantiles possible. As

Lady Purbeck she gave land adjoining the Common for a site for the chapel in 1676. She and her steward planned the building sites on Mount Sion in the 1680s. In 1703 four acres was set aside for a grove for the use of the inhabitants and visitors. Despite its financial embarrassment the family did much to create the amenities of the spa. It was helped by a national projector based in London, Thomas Neale, Master of the Mint and developer of Shadwell and the Seven Dials in London among numerous schemes, who bought the manor of Rusthall, and with Thomas Janson created the Walks. According to J.H. Thomas he built several shops and suffered a loss of about £2,000 in the fire. About 1682 he borrowed £2,000 from Thomas Dashwood, a London merchant, and in 1683 another £1,000; as he did not pay the interest, £3,925 was owed in the end and he was forced to assign all his Tunbridge Wells Estate, presumably including his 1686 lease of land on Mount Sion, to Dashwood in 1690.[22]

There were probably at least half a dozen people in the 1680s and 1690s who leased several large land plots either on the Walks, or on Mount Sion or Mount Ephraim and built on them extensively, perhaps sub-leasing the remaining land. On the Walks Thomas Ashenhurst, a 'gentleman' from Lambeth, perhaps a lawyer, built many of the shops with lodging rooms above them which were erected after the fire of 1688. They included the Royal Oak Lottery, the Hazard or Playroom, and seven shops on the Upper Walk, and 10 butchers' shops in the row opposite. He held

13 *Three detached houses adjoining the Common which were built on the former Inhams heath leased by Viscountess Purbeck after 1684; the house on the left is Rock Villa or Thackeray's house, with an early 18th-century façade.*

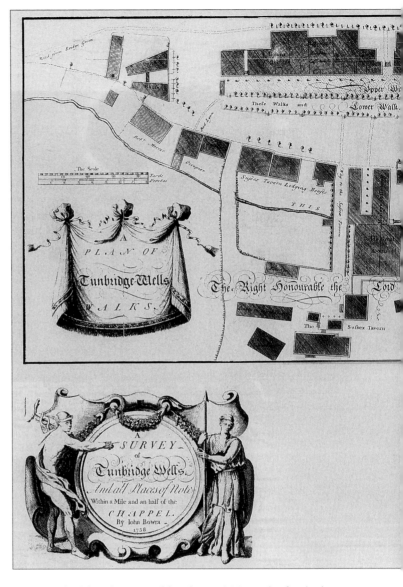

them on building leases, and by about 1700 was by far the largest lessee on the Walks, paying £115 out of a total estate rental of £349 4s. 6d. He also built or leased lodging houses on the hills.[23]

On Culverden one of the largest owners and builders was Sir Thomas Janson. As Neale's agent on the Walks he may have laid out the building plots alongside the Walks. Richard Constable's lease of the manor of Rusthall and his buildings on the Walks in the 1670s have been mentioned. He held the earliest lease on Mount Ephraim, of 19 acres and was the largest lessee on Mount Sion, taking about 50 acres between November 1684 and May 1687, much of which was sub-leased. Although the bowling green and the later Murray House were on his land, the extent to which

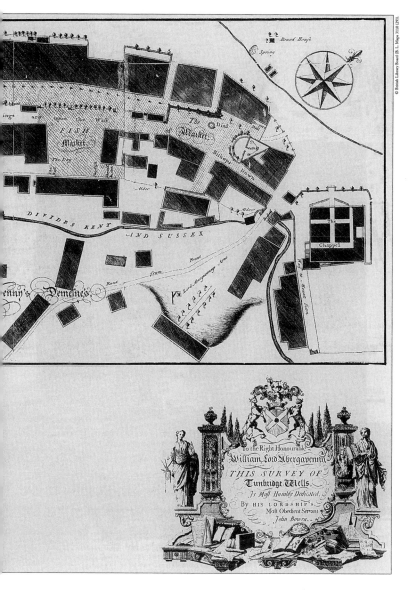

On the map:
Round House
Spring
FISH Market
The Market
Dial
Bishops Down
Alder
DIVIDES KENT AND SUSSEX
Frant
From
Road
Lord Abergavenny Arms
The Chappel
enny's Demesne

To the Right Honourable
William, Lord Abergavenny,
THIS SURVEY OF
Tunbridge Wells
Is Most Humbly Dedicated.
BY HIS LORDSHIP'S
Most Obedient Servant
John Bowra.

© British Library Board (B. L. Maps 3110 (29)).

14 *Plan of the Pantiles in 1738 by Bowra.*

he was a builder on Mount Ephraim and Mount Sion is uncertain. The sparse evidence suggests that he was a most influential early projector. Of similar importance was Thomas Weller, steward of the Rusthall and Southfrith manors, who built a shop on the Walks, several houses on the Southfrith demesne near the chapel, and other tenements at Culverden. The activities of Constable and Weller emphasise the key role of local people in initiating building.

Most of the builders erected only one or two houses. On the Walks in 1685 and 1686 Thomas Neale let 12 small plots, mostly intended for single shops, all to different people. John Fulman and Richard Dorsett on Mount Ephraim and Philip

15 *The back of a house fronting the High Street, built by Edward Martin, a joiner, on land leased from Viscountess Purbeck in 1684 (Farthing, Mount Sion).*

16 *The Grove on Mount Sion, created in 1703 by the landowner as a park for visitors and residents.*

Seale on Mount Sion, were builders on this smaller scale. Some speculated with little or no capital, and soon disposed of their leases at a profit. Others raised mortgages locally or in London to finish the work. In 1686 Gabriel Tomkin, a local bricklayer, leased four acres probably on Mount Sion. Lacking the money to begin building, he borrowed £50 from a Frant yeoman, Thomas Jeffery; then, needing more money to proceed, he borrowed £100 from Thomas Heywood, a Westminster 'gentleman' who may have been a lawyer, in February 1689. However, by Michaelmas the house was still unfinished, no interest had been paid on the mortgage, and Heywood sought a writ of ejectment. Finally new mortgagees were found in London who paid both the ground rent and the cost of completion.[24]

Although several houses on the Walks were erected by Londoners, such as Samuel Rose of Exeter Exchange in the Strand and William Pett of Allhallows Lombard Street, most of the small builders were local people.[25] Thus the land and planning of the development of the town were provided by the local landowners; while much of the larger-scale building was done by professional men and merchants from London, many of the shops and lodging houses were the work of local tradesmen and craftmen. The diverse origin of the builders and the speed with which houses were erected, show that property at the Wells was regarded as a fine speculative investment.

II The New Community

The Keepers of the Lodging Houses and the Shopkeepers

Building was principally to serve the visitors to the Wells in the summer season. A chief source of potential wealth was the lodging houses. Contemporary reports about accommodation varied. When Celia Fiennes visited the settlement in 1697 the boom was at its height: 'they have made the Wells very commodious by the many good buildings all about it and two or three mile around, which are lodgings for the company that drinke the waters, and they have encreased their buildings so much that makes them very cheape'. On the other hand 20 years later a Ned Ward found that 'lodgings are so dear and scarce that a Beau is sometimes glad of a Barn, and a Lady of Honour content to be in a garret. The horses being commonly put to grass, for the servants to lie in a Stable.' £1 5s. may have been a normal weekly charge for lodging a single person and is the amount Thomas Wilson DD agreed to pay 'at one Knights at the foot of Mount Sion' when he stayed on 14 July 1736. Naturally, families and those with servants were charged several pounds. There were separate payments for the use of the kitchen and the stables.[26]

Clearly lodging housekeepers found the 'well season' profitable: on 9 October 1695, at the end of the season when the visitors had left, Bridget, the wife of Thomas Witherden found that she had made £71 15s. during the summer, of which £48 was left after the servants' wages, taxes and repairs had been paid. Katherine, sister of Thomas Ashenhurst, let his 'two great lodging houses', and Jordan's House on Mount Sion between 1704 and 1707, for which the accounts have survived. In 1706 she was able to hand over a net profit of £50 from her total receipts of £180 9s.; her largest payments had been £38 8s. for ground rent, £31 17s. 11d. for taxation, and £38 for fodder; servants' wages and household equipment cost considerably less. Probably the provision of fodder in the stable was usually treated as a source of profit by the lodging housekeepers, for a visitor in 1690 remarked that 'they will not allow any lodger to buy his own hay or oats'; and out of Katherine Ashenhurst's gross profit of £180 9s. in 1706, £56 11s. or almost one third was described as coming from her stables. Her net profit as a percentage averaged 30 per cent in 1704-7, a large amount.[27]

It was the fashion for the visitors to buy their food from the stalls kept by the local people on the Walks. According to Celia Fiennes:

> All the people buy their own provision at the Market which is just by the Wells and furnish'd with great plenty of all sorts flesh, fowle and fish; … The country people come with all their back yard and barne door affords, to supply them with, and their gardens and orchards which makes the markets well stored and provisione cheape; which the Gentry takes as a diversion while drinking the waters to go and buy their dinners it being every day's market.

The local people were tempted to overcharge wealthy buyers. The frequent mention of the profits of the kitchen in Katherine Ashenhurst's accounts may imply that some of the visiting households cooked for themselves. A visiting family took a whole house or just one or two rooms. Buying a house was a rarity at this time.[28]

The shops, principally on the Walks, were the other chief source of profit. Fiennes found them 'full of all sorts of toys, silver and china'. Shopkeepers in different trades at about 1700 have already been mentioned. Many of them dealt in specialised, luxury goods for fashionable society; this was different from the normal small town of the period such as Tonbridge where the tradespeople served only the strictly practical needs of an agricultural society. The demand for souvenirs was met by 'Tunbridge Ware', a delicate woodwork, which was in vogue at the Wells from the beginning. Fiennes found the shops full of it, being that 'which this place is noted for'. The centre of this manufacture almost from the start was Mount Ephraim: a deed of 1737 mentions, among other houses, four messuages with 'workshops' (an unusual description), several turners, and a Simon Wise whose family was connected with the industry by tradition from this period.[29]

A further source of income were the public rooms where the company met for amusement and diversion. On the Walks Fiennes saw 'two large coffee houses for tea, chocolate, etc., and two rooms for the Lottery and Hazard board'. The bowling greens on Mounts Sion and Ephraim followed those at Rusthall and Southborough, with dancing later in the day and by 1738 there was horse racing on the Common, supported by the lord of the manor. Probably one of the largest undertakings were the fish ponds on Mount Ephraim, with gardens 'laid out in a pretty rural taste'. According to Burr, while the managers maintained its decency it was a principal place of diversion; but by his time it had decayed, through 'low company' being admitted. Although drinking at the wells on the Pantiles was regarded as the main source of health, and water was bottled for drinking in lodgings and even in London, a new fashion for coldbathing led to a bath inside a house with a decorative grotto being opened at Rusthall in 1708 by James Long of Marylebone. A shortlived bath and drinking well was created about 1750 on the edge of the Common by the Pantiles. Clearly the temptation to compete with existing amenities was too great.[30]

17 *Tunbridge Ware was the one manufacture associated particularly with the town; it was made in workshops on Mount Ephraim and in other places until the 1920s.*

The Early Inhabitants

According to tradition not only the visitors but also the tradespeople and lodging housekeepers abandoned the Wells in the early autumn, only returning at the beginning of the next season in May. Thus Sprange's *Directory* of 1816 wrote that after Michaelmas 'the tradespeople themselves migrated, the taverns were closed, the chapel service discontinued, and the place remained a desert, 'till the following spring'. This is only partly true. The Wells was built and exploited by Londoners, and by people living elsewhere in the district for whom the entertainment of the visitors was a secondary source of income. Several of the Londoners with shops on the Pantiles may have shut their London premises in May, and followed fashionable society to the Wells. Local tradespeople and

18 *View of King Charles Church in 1830. Built in 1676-96, it was the first church and is shown here with a turret and clock of 1760.*

farmers kept shops and lodging houses as a potentially profitable sideline. William Latter, tenant of the principal inn in Tonbridge, the *Rose and Crown*, had a large lodging house at the Wells when he died in 1728. John Jeffery, a wealthy local farmer, kept two lodging houses in 1708. Yet from the first, tradespeople lived at the Wells for the whole year. In the Tonbridge parish registers there were references to inhabitants from the 1680s: a daughter of John Skinner 'of the Wells' was baptised on 1 April 1687, and William Edwards 'of the Wells' was buried on 1 December 1691 – neither event took place in the summer months. A little is known about several of these early inhabitants. Mary Cooke, a mercer's widow, had a house and shop and seven acres which she farmed, four messuages and four acres on Culverden, besides the 'mansion house which I keep in my own hands for lodgers in the summer'. On Mount Sion Nicholas Wood, fellmonger and small farmer, had in 1724 'of late expended considerable money in building an addition to the house I now live in and furnished to make it complete for a lodging house'; brewhouses, coachhouses, workhouses and stables, with a garden, orchard and four pieces of land were attached. He also owned the Great House let to Philip Seale, the glazier, three other lodging houses in the hands of other tenants, and a shop on the Pantiles for the sale of his gloves. On a smaller scale his neighbour, Philip Seale, owned a lodging house, a two-acre field, two stables, a hay house and a meadow, as well as a shop on the Walks. Like hotelkeepers and shopkeepers at seaside resorts today, the income of these earliest inhabitants came mainly from the summer visitors; but they might add to their livelihood by following a trade of use to local people. Many had both a shop and one or two lodging houses; like craftsmen in small country towns and villages they often also kept livestock.[31]

The first chapels were built by subscriptions of the visitors primarily for their own use. The Anglican building was named King Charles the Martyr in honour of Stuart patronage of the Wells. It was erected in 1676-78, extended in about 1682 and doubled in 1688-96 because of growing numbers, producing an almost square-shaped layout, all in brick. Although plain outside, the plaster ceilings with its domes by John Wetherel and the Londoner Henry Doogood are glorious. The total cost was £2,278. According to Fuller, Thomas Neale was probably inspired to attract and organise the visitors before the shops and houses were built. The 2,526 subscribers included royalty, aristocrats, knights, known dissenters and Roman Catholics and 239 MPs, many of whom only visited once or twice. The minister was supported by the company, the chapel at first being closed during the winter. There was also a Presbyterian congregation from the early 1690s, the minister being paid by the visitors. Its meeting was allowed by the Toleration Act of 1689. A brick chapel with round-headed windows opened on Mount Sion in 1720.[32]

19 *A section of the splendid plaster ceiling of King Charles Church, showing the domes and surrounding decorations.*

With the beginning of a settled community from the 1690s, King Charles Chapel and later the Presbyterian Chapel were attended by local tradespeople. Long before 1713 a charity school attached to King Charles Chapel was set up by the visitors for the inhabitants of the Wells and of the neighbourhood, the schoolmaster being paid £24 and £2 for firing annually. Finally in 1716 a congregation of Baptists, which had been meeting locally since about 1646, settled permanently in the town, first on Mount Sion and then on Mount Ephraim. Its chapel was the first belonging purely to townspeople, and few visitors ever seem to have attended it.

The town had no government of its own, the inhabitants paying church, poor and highway rates to whichever of the three parishes they lived in. The vestry of King Charles Chapel consisted of visitors who supported the minister and the school and took responsibility for the Pantiles; the latter involved planting and cutting trees, providing lamps and benches, keeping horses off the Lower Walk, paying a sweeper and in 1729 supplying a cage for vagrants and beggars.[33] By 1740 the new community was well established. As well as the schoolmaster, clergyman and apothecary, there were one or two attorneys. Many of its families had been resident or associated with the settlement since the 1680s and 1690s: the Brett family still owned houses on Mount Sion on land leased to the London apothecary John Brett in 1690; the Seale family who had come in 1687 and the Woods who were there in the 1690s were prominent as tradesmen and lodging housekeepers. Several of them had become linked by marriage, such as the Frys, Seales and Mercers, and Waggons at Culverden. The community was like that of any other little town, its families strongly rooted in the district. Although many of their descendants were to survive among the tradespeople of succeeding generations, the character of the community was to begin to change with the advent in the late 18th century of a resident leisured class of retired businessmen, professional men and single women who were, naturally, rarely natives.[34]

III The Rise of the Residential Town, 1740-1800

The Visitors, the Immigrants and their Daily Lives

The face of the town stayed the same in the 60 years after 1740. A few houses were built in brick between Mount Sion and Culverden, and other houses, especially on Mount Ephraim, were improved or enlarged. It was still in the form of three villages, with the Pantiles remaining the social and commercial centre. While the population did not rise above 1,200 by 1800, the summer visitors were joined by a leisured class who settled for health reasons and retirement. Although the town lacked a local authority, it was one of the first to have a fire brigade, in 1794, the engine and its house being paid for by the Sun Fire Office and 71 local people and the freeholders of Rusthall Manor.[35]

The Wells was at the height of its reputation as a spa until the 1760s and 1770s. Count Grammont described it about 1700 as 'in place of all Europe the most rural and simple, and yet, at the same time, the most entertaining and agreeable', and as 'the general rendezvous of all the gay and handsome of both sexes'. While Epsom, which was nearer to London, attracted the merchants and tradespeople, visitors to the Wells were predominantly the royalty, aristocracy and gentry, and those who wished to belong to them. They included leading politicians and writers, and travellers who described its social life. Two Princes of Wales and Princess Amelia

20 *Richard 'Beau' Nash who set himself up as Master of Ceremonies from 1735.*

21 *The formidable Sarah Porter, whom Nash used as a touter to gain subscriptions from visitors.*

visited in the early and mid-18th century. The season alternated with that of Bath where the environment was a town. A character in a play of 1703 remarked rather caustically of the company in an amusing way: 'like most publick assemblies, a Medly of all sorts, Fops majestick and diminutive, from the long flaxen Wig with a splendid Equipage, to the Merchant's Spruce Prentice that's always mighty neat about the Legs; Squires come to Court some fine Town-Lady, and Town-Sparks to pick up a Russet-Gown'. People of different backgrounds mixed informally, their number reaching 900 in the first six weeks of July and August 1736. The actor went on to remark: 'Beaus Raffle and Dance – Citts play at Nine-Pins, Bowls and Backgammon – Rakes scoure the Walks, Bully the Shopkeepers, and beat the Fiddlers. Men of Wit rally over Claret, and Fools get to the Royal-Oak Lottery, where you may lose Fifty Guinea's in a Moment'. Both men and women enjoyed the gaming tables; as it was written in 1696: 'the town [London] very empty and no sign of money everywhere, but at the Bath and Tunbridge, where the ladies shake the elbow'.[36]

In the beginning, social life was uncontrolled. From the 1720s attempts were made to limit gambling; thus Kent quarter sessions at Maidstone in 1729 tried to end unlawful games – fair chance, faro and ace of hearts. By 1725 a remarkable woman, Bell Causey, was 'absolute governess' of the gaming-room, according to Phyllis Hembry. Between 1735 and 1755 Richard 'Beau' Nash from Bath developed a social code as Master of Ceremonies, arranging entertainments such as the music by a London band and the routine of the twice-weekly public balls. He even expected attendance at religious services twice a day. Subscriptions were fixed for bell-ringing, the orchestra, the water-dippers and admission to balls and card assemblies; Nash had a forceful woman, Sarah Porter, who touted newcomers for the various sums. He was followed by a succession of masters of ceremonies. Their social management reduced the wild and undisciplined character of some of the company. Burr in 1766 gave a perhaps rather idealised account of daily life: after drinking the waters in the early morning, most of the company breakfasted in their lodgings; then many attended chapel and spent the morning talking on the Upper Walk or visiting the milliners, jewellers and the bookshop with music in the background; after dinner they are on the Walk in their best clothes with music again; after meeting for tea there was card playing and gaming and, twice weekly, balls in the assembly rooms between six and eleven o'clock. Other entertainments were concerts, visits to the High Rocks, lectures, country excursions and horse races. Plays were put on by touring groups for a few weeks in the summer, with larger houses being improvised as temporary theatres. The most notable showwoman was Sarah Baker, whose company may have been performing from the 1770s plays well-known or unknown today mixed with music, singing and dancing.[37]

Notable people continued to flock to the Wells. An anonymous writer on 30 July 1773 remarked that 'this place is extremely full ... Among the company now down are the Dukes of Leeds and Dorset, Earl Tyrconnel and Lady, Lord Mountmorris, Sir John Seabright, Sir Thomas Wilson, etc., etc.'. Elizabeth Montagu, Samuel Richardson, Fanny Burney and other celebrated names corresponded from there, and leading politicians and their wives were among the company. Mrs Montagu wrote to her husband in July 1753: 'Mr Fox and Lady Caroline are come here for a few days, as are Ld and Lady Hillesborough: as pleasure not health is their object they will not stay long. I was at the Ball last night ... Mr Pitt goes tomorrow to Hastings for two days ...'.[38]

By the 1780s some of the gaiety of its life had disappeared, and the company grew more select and sedate. While it reflected a change in English society in general, the seaside resorts were attracting a growing number of visitors in the summer. After 1789 Weymouth constantly welcomed George III and his court, and Brighton became prominent under the patronage of the Prince of Wales and his set. Younger and more lively people were drawn from the Wells to Brighton. As Amsinck wrote in 1810, though probably exaggerating, 'in the zenith of its prosperity the fashionable mixture was considerable, and every vice reigned with uninterrupted sway'; now it had a reputation for 'good and select company'; 'the fashionable parts of the company ... seek rather the pleasures of retirement and the comforts of moderate

22 *High Rocks was a favourite attraction for visitors who rode or walked there in the later 18th century.*

society, than of dissipation'. Yet though the town was quieter and no longer attracting the wilder elements of upper-class society, it was still well attended by summer visitors. After Lord North ceased to be Prime Minister he used to stay at the bottom of Mount Sion, and Lord Chief Justice Mansfield also visited in the 1780s. On the Parade it was fashionable to attend chapel in the morning, then listen to the music and join the thickening crowd on the Upper Walk until Amsinck's day.[39]

23 *Toad Rock on the Common, one of the favourite walking or riding attractions of the visitors.*

It was partly because of its changing social life that the Wells began to attract permanent leisured residents. They also came for the same reasons as some of the visitors, for their health, to drink the waters or enjoy the healthy climate. There was also the environment, 'romantic, rural, rugged, and with a vast variety of different views ... as agreeable and pleasant a place as ever I saw' as a visitor remarked in 1767. The countryside was ideal for walks and rides, and the guide books described the country houses that could be visited. The town was nearer London than was Bath: in 1767 the journey of under 40 miles took five or five and a half hours by fly, and eight hours by stagecoach. Furthermore, of great importance was the fact that life was cheaper in the Wells than in London. The often middle-aged and elderly new inhabitants in turn influenced social life, perhaps by avoiding the daily routine on the Pantiles.[40]

There had been one or two gentry near the Wells since 1700, yet they were there principally as landowners. One of the earliest was William Strong, who bought Calverley Lodge and about 200 acres from the Earl of Buckingham in 1702. A trustee of the chapel, at his death he left two farms near Pembury village, the income from which was to be used partly to apprentice a scholar of the charity school. A larger landowner was George Kelley, a wealthy physician from Portsmouth, who married Johanna Cock of Mount Ephraim in 1743. He paid £12,000 for the manor of Rusthall and the houses on the Walks, and nearly £7,000 for houses on Mount Ephraim, and small farms and fields totalling 250 acres elsewhere in Speldhurst. His total rental was nearly £1,100. He also leased and farmed some land; when he died in 1772 he had 25 acres under crops, and was breeding a few sheep and cattle. He was active in local and county affairs, as a magistrate, a leading trustee of the chapel, and as Sheriff of Kent in 1762. After his death his family kept the estate and were notable residents.[41]

The influx of retired professional and business men and their families, and single gentlewomen began about the 1770s. They normally bought one or two houses. Several of them may be mentioned. Martin Yorke was the son of a Northamptonshire clergyman, who became a major in the service of the East India Company. Returning from India with a fortune and in poor health he settled at the Wells, where he lived for the last 20 years of his life. A local guide book of 1780 mentions the 'great improvements' he had made to his house on Mount Ephraim 'now the entire residence of himself and his family'. Elsewhere on Mount Ephraim the widow of a bishop of Worcester, a Mrs Johnson, had lately bought the Castle Houses; one of them she had altered, and similarly 'now makes it her chief place of residence'. On the top of Mount Sion, significantly in a house on the site of the old bowling green and assembly room, lived Richard Cumberland. He had been driven from London with its more costly lifestyle when he lost public office. Despite his prodigious output of plays, he was active in local affairs, raising a corps of volunteer infantry during the French Wars. Lord Viscount Boyne and Sir George Buggin built mansions on Mout Ephraim about 1800, and were magistrates.[42]

24 *Sarah Jennings, Duchess of Marlborough. She visited the Wells continually in the 1720s and '30s.*

Many people came as summer residents year after year. In 1780 there was a 'noble modern brick house' on Mount Pleasant which 'the Duke of Leeds has honoured with his residence for several years past'. Joseph Hiller, a woollen-draper of Southwark, held Chancellors House on Mount Ephraim in 1770. It was then let to Sir Richard Heron of Grosvenor Square, who finally bought it in 1785. In a list of 26 men or women or couples of independent means in 1803, nine had titles and four were retired soldiers. These new inhabitants brought wealth to the town, providing shopkeepers with a livelihood all the year. Contemporaries noted their munificence, by which 'the neighbouring poor are greatly relieved, and kept in full employ: and the tradespeople likewise reap benefit extraordinary during the winter season'.[43]

Some of the tradespeople and professional men who were property owners were descended from earlier inhabitants while others were immigrants. A lodging house later known as Fairlawn House in Mount Sion Road built by Thomas Scoones, a yeoman, before 1702, passed to his daughter and son-in-law Richard Jeffery, which they held until they died in 1770; their granddaughter, Ann Jeffery, who was 17 in 1790 and heiress to it, as well as much property in London and Pembury and a large income from Funds, married a Welshman, the Rev. Thomas Stephens, who had been the incumbent at King Charles before moving to Frant; they let the house and lived at Great Lodge, Pembury and in Devonshire Place, west London.[44]

Mount Ephraim was now favoured, rather than Mount Sion, for the magnificence of its view and retired position. As a result this part of the town, which a generation earlier was being neglected by visitors owing to its distance from the wells, received a new lease of life. While few new houses appeared, all along the edge of the Common the old buildings were being improved.

The Shops and the Lodging Houses

At the division of the Walks Estate in 1739, a block of some of the best public rooms and shops passed to the freeholders. In 1739 it was worth £366 10s., and was held by 10 tenants. Between 1770 and 1789 the rental was between £360 and £330 a year, thereafter falling to a little over £300. The Great Rooms were some of the principal public rooms on the Pantiles, and were let for £190 in 1770.[45]

The value of the lord's share of the Walks Estate, consisting of some 50 shops and taverns at the time of the partition, was £652 11s. While in 1741 the receiver accounted for a rent of £652

2s. 3d., owing to one or two empty houses during the next four years the rent was about £50 lower. During 1741 expenditure was as follows:

> William Wood [steward] yearly allowance for supervising repairs, looking after the tenants, collecting the heriots [fines payable on death and inheritance] etc. £20
> Repairs £97 1s 8d
> Receiver's salary £35
> Receiver for going to Tunbridge Wells to hold the audit and give directions about repairs £20 10s
> Money spent on dinner and wine for the tenants as usual at the audit etc. £8 15s 6d
>
> ————
>
> Total £181 7s 2d

Payments were quite similar in the next four years, except for £473 12s. 4d. in 1744 for extensive rebuilding. The rents rose a little to £728 7s. 6d. in 1785 and £749 18s. 6d. in 1790, and then jumped to £929 1s. 2d. in 1800 as prices rose.[46]

Forty-six tradesmen were listed in a rental of the Walks Estate belonging to the lord in 1774. Some of the shops served the visitors and the few leisured residents who had already arrived. There were five 'toy shops' selling Tunbridge Ware, a bookseller, pastry cook, two perfumers and two milliners. There was also a billiard room and a coffee house. The other shopkeepers were typical of any country town: they included an apothecary, two barbers, three grocers, a baker, a brewer, three butchers, two shoemakers, two tailors, a smith, an ironmonger and a saddler. Two people were described as lodging housekeepers and some of the shopkeepers let upper rooms for lodgings. There were also five victuallers and the occupier of the Gloucester Tavern. One or two of the shopkeepers selling luxuries came from London for the summer, and some probably shut at the end of the season; however, many stayed open throughout the year to serve local people, including neighbouring farmers. Some were still small farmers themselves. A few helped to clear several hundred acres of heath and forest on the south of the town in the demesnes of Lord Abergavenny; in 1777 David Langridge, a wheelwright in the town, was leased 27 acres for 21 years on condition that he improved and enclosed it. The commercial and social importance of the Pantiles was confirmed when subscriptions totalling £711 paid for the replacement of the tile paving by Purbeck stone flagging in 1793; it was called the Parade until the old name was revived in 1887.[47]

Elsewhere the majority of the houses had lodging rooms. There were 68 in 1780: 16 lay along Mount Ephraim, 13 on the eastern edge of the Common, two on Mount Pleasant, and no less than 37 on Mount Sion and near the chapel. The number rose to 86 in 1801. With new inhabitants particularly occupying houses on Mount Ephraim, the supremacy of Mount Sion as a centre for lodgings was confirmed.[48]

Tunbridge Ware was made mainly in workshops on Mount Ephraim, and sold on the Pantiles. Turners used lignum vitae imported from the Americas, whitewoods such as holly and sycamore and brown woods such as cherry, plum and yew to make goblets, bowls, cups and other items. By the late 18th century boxes for writing, sewing, dressing and storage of tea, cosmetics and smelling salts became more important. Some were veneered, or by the 1790s, decorated with prints. It is interesting that many of these items made in the town's first industry were intended for women. In 1803 there were eight manufacturers and dealers. By then the professions too were becoming well established; three attorneys included John Stone, who had settled in 1797 and whose family were to be local solicitors for nearly 200 years. There were two apothecaries and two doctors, though one, Dr Mayo, practised in London in winter. The schoomaster had his salary raised to £30 in 1771 and £45 in 1811 and was provided with a wainscotted anti-gallery in the chapel to teach the children all the year in 1787. The chapel had a resident clergyman from 1729; in 1766 there were said to be daily services in season and three a week in winter and although the clergyman's salary was then said to be the respectable £200, at least in 1784 the contributions on which it was based were inadequate.[49]

IV The Beginning of Expansion, 1800-1835

The Renewal of the Parade, the Common, Mount Sion and Mount Ephraim

From about 1800, when the population was around 1,200, the town grew rapidly. In 1831 it had 5,929 inhabitants and in 1841 8,302. By then it had far surpassed in size nearly all the inland Kentish market towns, including Tonbridge. It grew ever more popular as a home for older leisured people, and tradesmen and labourers increased correspondingly. While an exodus to the continent occurred after 1815 the number of summer visitors also grew to about 5,000 in 1840, helped by better roads and more comfortable coaches. There were 138 lodging houses in 1816 and 188 in 1822. The future Queen Victoria and her mother, the Duchess of Kent, came at least five times between 1822 and 1835, attending King Charles Chapel, going for rides and doing good works. Melville mentioned some of the visits of Mary Berry between 1807 and 1812: on 17 August 1812 when the news of the Salamanca victory arrived 'there was a generation illumination … The

25 *Princess Victoria and the Duchess of Kent returning from a donkey ride in 1822, with Jordan Place used as an 'original manufactory of Tunbridge ware' and shop by 'Burrows'.*

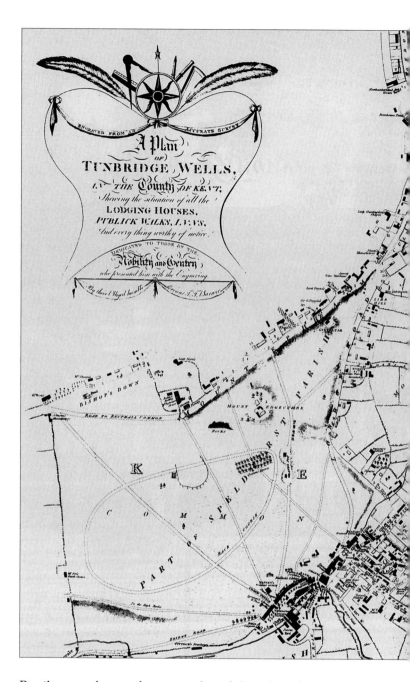

26 *Map of Tunbridge Wells in 1806 by Barrow, showing little more building than that in 1738.*

Pantiles were decorated very prettily with branches of ash mixed with flowers and laurels'. The Duke of Sussex spent some months there in 1820 when George Keppel stayed with him and he went to a ball 'at the Assembly Rooms' with Lord Albemarle. Thackeray as a schoolboy spent his summer holidays there in 1823. The many *Guides* and *Directories* were signs of the town's attractions. Rebuilding took place on the Parade and more houses appeared on Mount Sion and Mount Ephraim. A vast building scheme

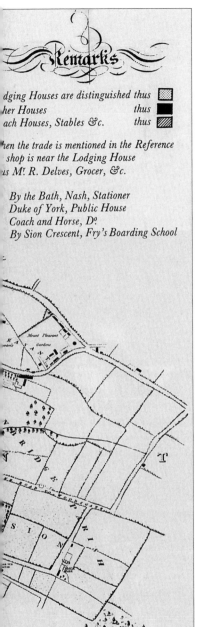

called the Calverley Estate was developed from 1829 to the north of Mount Pleasant, and many short streets lined with houses were opened around it.[50]

Much evidence has survived about the history of the Parade between the 1800s and the 1830s. The rent of the estate of the freeholders of the Manor of Rusthall was generally just under £300. It stayed level despite the rise of about 40 per cent in property values between 1790 and 1815. This was caused by the fall in the rent of the Great Rooms from £190 in 1770 to £91 in 1821, because long daily public appearances stopped being so popular with visitors. The rents of the rest of the properties, which were shops, rose a little over the same time. Their failure to grow appreciably in value was caused by the long pause in the growth of the town before 1800, and then the decline in the commercial importance of the Parade as the town expanded northwards.

Usually most of the income was distributed to the freeholders as dividends, from £40 to £60 being spent on items such as land tax, insurance, the salaries of officials and minor repairs. Structural repairs were the owners' responsibility, and every few years disbursements might reach £100. While in 1777 large scale alterations had cost £347 11s. 11d., and four years later £449 6s. 5d., similar expenditure was not incurred until 1822. At a meeting of freeholders on 12 February, a surveyor named John Montier was asked to examine the premises, and particularly the roofs and foundations. He was reminded that all ornamental repairs, such as painting, plastering and whitewashing, were to be done by the tenants. Following his report a fortnight later, the freeholders decided to invite tenders for the work, and that placards should be widely circulated round Tonbridge town and the Wells. On 11 March they accepted tenders from Douch and Bellingham for the carpenters' and smiths' work at £248, subject to proper security for fulfilment of the contract, from Cripps for masons' and bricklayers' work at £140, and from Thomas Taylor for plumbers, painters and glaziers' work at £27 17s. 6d. Three freeholders, Joseph and Thomas Delves, and Ezra Seamer, were to superintend the work, and authorise additional expenditure when absolutely necessary. In the event only £19 5s. more was needed, and the total bill, with £20 for the surveyor, was £455 2s. 6d.

Among the maintenance tasks to which the tenants were bound in their leases was one for treating the outside wood and iron every seven years with 'three good coats of oil paint'. Occasionally the tenants undertook improvements: thus in 1808 the lease of a house and shop to a linen-draper, Edward Palmer, stated that he had just spent £300 on new building. The officials of the estate were two trustees, usually local gentry, two stewards and a clerk or secretary. Except for extraordinary business the freeholders met each Michaelmas. Here leases were granted, almost always for 21 years, proposed alterations by the tenants were carefully regulated or rejected, and officials were appointed and their salaries revised.[51]

On the estate of the lord of the manor rents rose sharply between 1790 and 1800, as has been seen. They continued to grow until 1815: 1790, £749 18s. 6d.; 1800, £929 1s. 2d.; 1805, £970 7s. 6d.; 1810, £1,003 8s.; 1815, £1,155 2s.; 1820, £1,133 1s.; 1835, £1,292 6s. There was a rise from £1,011 15s. in 1812 to £1,155 1s. between 1812 and 1813, owing to new rent for the Baths. The other changes came from rents of one or two new properties, such as a 'shop under the music gallery' in 1813, and from minor increases on renewal of leases. Yet over the 80 years between 1740 and 1820 the alteration was relatively small, as in the case of the freeholders' Estate.

Although structural repairs were usually done by the lord of the manor, occasionally they were carried out by the tenants. In November 1833 the steward, William Scoones, told the lord about the dilapidated state of the buildings at the far end of the Parade, remarking that 'if nothing is done the buildings will take the law in their own hands and tumble down'. He recommended letting the houses on building leases. This was done, and two years later he could write that 'the Walks Estate has improved considerably and is still improving'; three tenants had rebuilt their houses, and three more had made great alterations.

An important change on the Parade was the erection of the Baths by Miss Shorey, a niece and heiress of George Kelley, between 1801 and 1805. It was a two-storey building, which replaced the hall erected in 1664 behind the wells, consisting of two large bathrooms on the ground floor and eight rooms on the first floor. There were cold and warm, vapour and shower baths. The comfortable rooms above were for the accommodation of invalids of modest means, wishing to try a regular course of bathing. According to a contemporary the Baths were 'in the first style of elegance and accommodation'; £76 7s. was paid for Wedgwood tiles for the inside of the baths, and £495 6s. 4d. to Francis Bernasconi of Alfred Place, Bedford Square, for plasterer's work. The total cost was over £4,000. At first Miss Shorey ran the Baths personally; an amusing letter has survived from the owner of baths in Brighton discussing how she might prevent two people using the same bath and only paying for one! After 1813 they were let for £120 a year, a low yield of under three per cent on the original outlay.

27 *The Bath House built by Elizabeth Shorey, lady of the manor of Rusthall and owner of two-thirds of the properties on the Parade in 1805.*

For the administration of the Walks Estate and the Manor of Rusthall the lords employed a bailiff, who lived at the Wells, and a steward from the firm of Scoones, attorneys in Tonbridge town. One of their duties was the care of the Common, as part

28 *The Duchess of Kent and Princess Victoria, who was 16 in 1835 on her last visit before she became Queen.*

29 *The Parade in 1827, showing the Bath House run by 'Hodgson', the Circulating Library on the left, a fruiterer's and other shops on the right.*

of the waste of the manor. Its scenic importance was now fully realised by the inhabitants. When in 1832 a scheme was proposed for erecting a railway from Penshurst to the Wells, to end on the Common, William Scoones remarked that due to the beauty and the purity of its air the Common was one of the great attractions to visitors: 'this beautiful Common has been aptly described as being of the same importance to Tunbridge Wells as the sea is to Hastings or Brighton'. Part of the bailiff's expenses were for watching the Common, cutting down unsafe trees and clearing the furze near the footpaths; a difficult task was to stop the destruction of the rest of the furze. On 19 October 1831 Scoones was written to in panic with a complaint about its burning at night: 'thus the chief beauty of the place is wantonly destroyed and the neighbourhood endangered'; his informant was the more concerned because 5 November was approaching![52]

In honour of Princess Victoria, on three or four days in February 1835 the freeholders with the lord paid for the planting of 132 elm, lime and sycamore trees in three rows on the Common. A procession led by a band marched onto the site on the first day; such a procession being typical of formal occasions. About 150 men, women and youngsters participated, followed by a dinner for 'upwards of 200' people; the new Royal Victoria Grove lay next to the grove planted in honour of Queen Anne's accession in 1702.

The groves symbolised in a way the debt owed by the inhabitants to all the visitors.[53]

In addition to the changes to the shops adjoining the Upper Walk, substantial improvements were made in the lower row of shops, taverns and lodging houses owned by the Earl of Abergavenny. The tenant of the principal building, once the Sussex Tavern and renamed in the 1830s the *Royal Victoria and Sussex Hotel*, spent £5,000 on alterations; a guide book of 1840 mentions its elegant frontage and its interior 'fitted up in the most complete manner for the reception of the nobility and gentry'. Besides the well and the Baths, the two assembly rooms were still used; and a small theatre which opened in the season, was created for £1,500 or £1,600 in 1802 by Sarah Baker, lasting until 1843. Public entertainment was slowly declining, with house parties becoming more common. The Parade still provided the amusements and the luxury retailers for the company.[54]

Mount Sion was becoming quite fashionable again as a lodging and residential area. In the 1830s the largest houses were still in their own grounds,

30 *Princess Victoria leaving by coach in 1834 with many townspeople watching; the* Royal Victoria and Sussex Hotel *and the Sussex Commercial House are shown.*

31 *The theatre on the Abergavenny side of the Parade, built by Sarah Baker in 1802.*

32 *Sion House, Mount Sion: a large lodging house with an early 19th-century façade, the elaborate portico being typical of the period.*

33 *Caxton House, Mount Sion, with an early 19th-century façade and typical portico and verandah.*

occupied by prominent townsmen such as propertied tradesmen like the Delves, solicitors such as Robert Foreman, and people of independent means such as Aretas Akers, a JP of Bellevue House, with their servants. Many houses were more closely packed and lived in by leisured people, tradesmen, craftsmen and labourers. Some of the gardens were used as building plots. At the bottom of the Mount Joseph and William Delves built Bedford Terrace in 1833; they were great-grandchildren of Richard Delves who came to Tunbridge Wells about 1750, had 10 children, owned 11 farms and was a butcher and lodging housekeeper according to Farthing. There was also rebuilding and new housing on Mount Ephraim, occupied by lodging housekeepers and hotelkeepers as well as one or two professional men and makers of Tunbridge Ware. The Hare and Hounds Tavern, much improved, became the *Mount Ephraim Hotel.* On both hills many houses were refronted in stucco, and sometimes adorned with bow windows.[55]

The New Estates

Nearly all the new housing was erected up to half a mile north of Mount Sion and about the same distance east of the Common, in which there was just a few scattered buildings adjoining a road. At least 10 owners, some being from families of tradespeople and some absentee, had fields there, and in the middle was 60 acres to the east of Mount Pleasant Road belonging to a local squire, Thomas Panuwell. Development began in the 1800s and rose to a peak between the late 1820s and 1835. While some of the owners laid out roads and building plots, others sold to developers to prepare estates. There was a mixture of sales and building leases of plots. When cottage tenements selling for £40 or £50 were expected, no covenants were imposed on builders. If the intended houses were substantial, worth £150 or £200 or more, building was controlled by the owner or developer. Some of the building owners or lessees were bricklayers or carpenters often intending a quick disposal, while others seeking a local investment contracted with craftsmen for the work. As usual much capital was borrowed in the form of mortgages.

Among the earliest schemes was the development in the 1800s of Pound Field on the north side of the road from Mount Pleasant to Pembury, later known as Hervey Town. On plots sold by the Earl of Bristol a Tunbridge-Ware maker, Thomas Burrows (died 1810), had nine cottages erected. Building on the Crown Field on the east of the road to Southborough is an example of unregulated development. It was bought by a local victualler named Henry Maynard, who began selling plots mostly beside new roads in 1813. By 1840 there were about 120 or 150 brick or weather-boarded tenements of four rooms, two up and two down, many in rows of six or seven dwellings and erected at various dates. The building owners included two labourers and the son of one of them who was a victualler. Again there were no covenants about building construction, nor any relating to drainage on the five-acre Windmill Field development between 1830 and 1838. The developer was a builder named Charles Cripps, who paid the former owner, John Stone, an attorney, a price of £1,535, which reflected some of its value for building. He laid out lanes and sold the regularly-shaped plots. Apart from the *Royal Oak Inn* and Mount Calverley Lodge which Cripps built for himself, and numbers 1 and 2 Park Place, adjoining the main road, the builders and speculators erected a gridiron pattern of 109 cottages in 22 rows. As the Calverley Estate was being built at the same time, this largely artisan housing was needed quickly. Poorer tradesmen, craftsmen and labourers such as laundresses, ostlers and servants lived on these estates.

From 1826 George T. Langridge was letting building plots at the bottom of Mount Pleasant on land he had inherited from his father, the wheelwright. In 1832 he leased land with a 145-foot frontage to Luke Long, a local innkeeper, for 70 years. Long agreed to build a terrace of eight houses within four years,

34 *An early 19th-century mansion in spacious grounds on Mount Ephraim.*

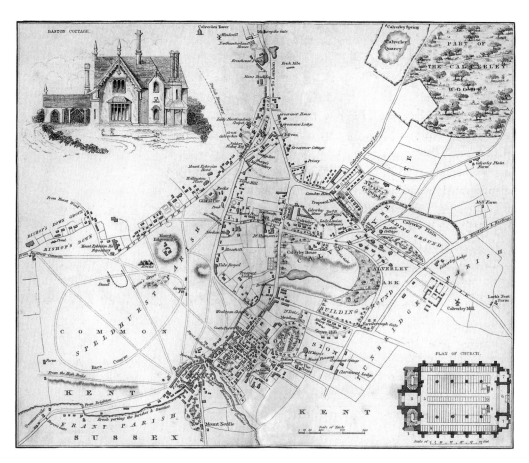

35 *Map of Tunbridge Wells in 1831 with the Calverley Estate in the process of being built, and the Pound Field, Crown Field, Langridge (including Edgar Terrace) and Windmill Field developments.*

according to plans approved by Langridge. Although he built two in 11 months, he then had to borrow £400 on mortgage from W.H. Lidbetter, a 'gentleman' who may have been an attorney. He was able to build three more houses by 1837, but then defaulted on his mortgage. Lidbetter undertook to build the rest, and the next year the eight houses were all erected. By 1840 the Langridge land had produced over 40 dwellings in terraces.

A drain in the road and drains linked to it from the houses were included in the covenants imposed on building owners by Henry Hopkins, a Maidstone timber merchant, who developed Hanover Road and Rock Villa Road from 1832, and by James Hockett Fry, a retired local butcher on the Grosvenor House Estate in 1835. Hopkins had just bought two acres for £1,500 as a speculation. According to a surviving title deed, one of his building owners in Hanover Road was a Mayfield schoolmaster, James Damper, who had to build a house worth at least £200 and not to carry on any offensive trade. The same covenants imposed on other purchasers produced a uniform row of houses which still stands. At the same time building also took place at the north end of the town, at the Lew, on land owned by John Gibb of Strood, an attorney, which was probably without any control by covenants.[56]

The death of Thomas Panuwell in 1824 and the inheritance of his properties by several heirs precipitated the sale of the Wells Estate in 1826. It was bought for £24,135 by John Ward of Devonshire Place and Holwood Park near Hayes in north-west Kent, probably a rich City merchant, who also bought some smaller properties in 1825-6 to form an estate of 874 acres; like other country gentlemen he was a J.P. and deputy lieutenant. His mansion at Holwood had been designed by an already well-known young architect, Decimus Burton, and he asked Burton to plan the development for building on the 60-acre site. Burton had been involved with the building of Regents Park and the existence of 60 acres in single ownership on the edge of the town allowed the layout of houses and parkland in a similar way; the houses on Mount Ephraim facing the Common with their splendid downward view also encouraged spacious planning. While terraces were usual in Georgian towns, detached and semi-detached villas were now becoming fashionable. To the east of the Mount Pleasant Road 26 acres of ornamental parkland was laid out; at its eastern end a row of 42 mostly detached villas were planned in an arc, though only 24 were built. To the north, at the west end, were 12 smaller three-storey terraced houses called Calverley Parade, and facing south a

36 *A view of the Common with a flock of sheep in the foreground and 19th-century houses on Mount Ephraim in the background.*

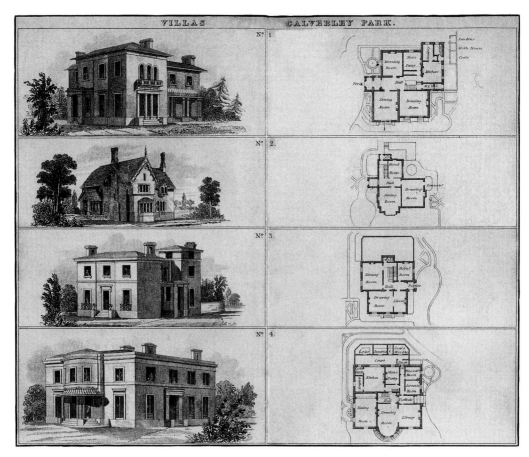

37 *Four of the villas on the Calverley Estate with ground plans, 1831.*

38 *One of the villas in Calverley Park built in the early 1830s.*

39 *Modern view of Calverley Park Crescent from the rear.*

row of four double villas called Calverley Terrace. Opposite the latter was a hotel and on the north side of the park a terraced crescent of 17 shops and lodgings of three storeys called Calverley Promenade. A hundred yards to the north lay the commercial centre, with a market place, inn and row of shops and houses, with other houses and four- and six-roomed cottages for poorer families behind. The elevations and even the internal layout of the houses on the estate were specified. The houses were built on 72-year leases, and the commercial row on 21-year terms. According to Whitbourn five of the villas were to be built annually, one costing not less than £1,800, two not less than £1,500, and two to be semi-detached costing at least £1,200.

The first leases for the Calverley Park villas and Calverley terraces, were made on 3 April 1829; the others followed later in 1829, 1831 and 1833. Much of the land was taken by Messrs Bramah of Pimlico, who had inherited the fortune made by a famous engineer and inventor, Joseph Bramah; capital made in manufacturing was now going into building, a not uncommon occurrence. Their workshops were near the site of the inn and the stone came from

the quarry on the estate. They assigned some of their holding and built extensively themselves, including the Promenade and some of the villas. Some of the houses in Calverley Parade were built by Decimus Burton and others by two local builders named Barrett; a William Scantlebury, carpenter and joiner, erected two villas and other houses. The estate was mostly built by 1836 and finished, except for the market place, in 1840. Retired men and women of independent means with up to eight or ten servants lived in many of the houses. The park and neighbouring houses contributed to the continued spacious layout of the town. However, the estate was too far from the town centre to be fully successful; the Promenade became houses as the shops were not needed, and the market place became the Town Hall in the 1840s. The town still had a higher proportion of substantial houses than in the typical important market town; the normal settlement depending on trade, had its housing built as near as possible to the shopping centre.[57]

40 *View of Calverley Park Promenade (now Calverley Crescent) intended for shops with lodging rooms above, 1860.*

41 *The commercial part of the Calverley Estate showing the Market Hall which became the Town Hall, the inn and row of substantial houses intended for shops and lodging accommodation, c.1840.*

Social Changes

The Parade continued to provide entertainments. After Mrs Baker a London actor named Dowton, who was her son-in-law, ran her Kentish theatres; he was followed by a comic singer and performer called Sloman until 1838, after which a decline in play-going led to their closure in 1843. The assembly rooms were used for concerts, balls and card playing; the two coffee houses (unusually one for men and one for women), the bookshops with lending libraries as well as the assembly rooms offered opportunities for leisurely conversation. The coldbaths at Rusthall were still patronised, there were tea gardens nearby, and a 'Great Bath House' was opened in the London Road in 1816. Entertainments varied between the boisterous and basic for artisans and labourers, many of whom were illiterate, and the quiet and cultured for the educated, especially women. On 26 August 1799 games on the Common were advertised to 'be given by the gentry visitants, to promote holyday happiness', including a match 'four men to smoke tobacco for a hat' and a run for 'young ladies' for 'a holland chemise, or linen convenience, of large dimensions'. In November 1820 when the King failed to get the Queen convicted of adultery

42 *The Common was used for several games, including cricket from the early 19th century.*

by Parliament, people were told that Richard Delves was going to give a bullock 'to be roasted on the Common, and … to distribute six butts of good old stingo, to drink her Majesty's health'. The town also had teachers of painting, languages and the piano. Donkey rides on the Common like those at Brighton were popular, as was archery among the women in the 1830s; an archery club was set up in Calverley land in 1834 and Rusthall had a society of lady archers. Racing on two days in August appealed to most people; after rowdy, drunken conduct in 1833 nearly led to races being abandoned, a determined effort to control the popular crowd and attract the gentry in 1834 led to 16,000 attending, including, unexpectedly, Princess Victoria on the second day.[58]

The Parade also continued to sell the Tunbridge Ware which reached its highest quality in the 1830s. Several new types were devised: miniature parquetry consisting of a veneer of tiny geometric forms; inlaid turnery produced by fixing shaped segments of contrasting woods together and working them on a lathe; and most importantly, tessellated mosaic ware, made using thin sticks of wood grouped in blocks then sawn through into slim veneers. A James Burrows invented the first two techniques and perhaps the last. He was one of a family making wares in the early 19th century, and the techniques were quickly adopted by other makers.[59]

The rapidly growing population developed the variety of institutions it needed. As King Charles the Martyr was a chapel of ease, marriages and burials were performed in the parish churches of Tonbridge, Speldhurst and Frant; there were baptisms in the chapel almost from the beginning. In England there was a rising religious revival and the need for another church now became acute. A

43 *Races on the Common for two days in August were an annual event.*

public meeting on 25 August 1824 confirmed that the chapel was quite inadequate owing to the great increase of buildings and population: 'a large proportion of the inhabitants of Tunbridge Wells have no place of worship on the Establishment, to which they may resort, and that in consequence thereof, some hundreds of the poorer classes never have the opportunity, and in fact never do enter a place of worship'. In short, an additional building was needed with extensive free admission to the lower classes, that is, without pew rents. There was also the practical need for a burial ground near the Wells.

Holy Trinity was built between 1827 and 1829, costing £10,591. The Duchess of Kent, with Princess Victoria attending, laid the foundation stone. It was a Gothic building designed by Decimus Burton, suitable for preaching, and in a dominating position at the top of Mount Pleasant. Eight hundred and eleven of the 1,427 seats were free. Like other new churches, it was built largely by private gifts: Lord Abergavenny subscribed £300, the minister of the chapel, Martin Benson, £200, and the lord of the manor of Rusthall and two other men £100 each, among the many contributors. There was a grant from the Church Building Commissioners who supported church building in growing towns. In 1833 it was assigned a separate ecclesiastical district, including the chapel and the whole town previously in Tonbridge parish: the first parish of Tunbridge Wells was created.[60]

44 *An 1831 view of Holy Trinity Church which was designed by Decimus Burton and built in 1827-9.*

Baptist and Presbyterian congregations existed since the 1690s, as already noted. By the 1800s their chapels had disappeared and been replaced by new buildings. In 1769 a large chapel at Culverden was founded by the Countess of Huntingdon and referred to as her Connexion. John Wesley preached several times, and in 1812 a Methodist Chapel was opened at the foot of Mount Sion; they had 500 and 350 members respectively in 1829 when dissenting congregations were counted, thus showing that they were well supported; some members would have come from neighbouring villages. The rapid expansion of the town in the 1830s was reflected in three new chapels. A visitor from Highbury, Thomas Wilson, established a Congregational Chapel for over £700 on Mount Sion in 1830. The Baptists built a chapel designed by their minister in Hanover Road for £1,265 and a Roman Catholic Chapel was founded in Grosvenor Road nearby. The strength of Nonconformity throughout the history of the town was in part due to the encouragement of the visitors and possibly, for some local people, the lack of a strong Anglican influence in the form of a parish church before 1833.[61]

The growing attention to religion was also seen in the Tonbridge and Tunbridge Wells Bible Society of 1812 and the Tonbridge and Tunbridge Wells Church Missionary Society in 1827. The Wells was thus still following the lead of the Tonbridge parish church. As the town was becoming sizeable, and was a spa

45 *An 1831 view of Holy Trinity Church from the east end and the Gothic Priory houses built in the 1820s.*

46 *The original wooden Countess of Huntingdon Connexion Chapel on Mount Ephraim built in 1769.*

47 *St Augustine's Roman Catholic Chapel in Grosvenor Road, 1839.*

with many prosperous inhabitants, one may assume that private acts of charity for the sick, orphans, the aged and even beggars abounded. Group activities included the Female School of Industry (1812) for teaching girls to read and write and training them for service, the Society for Lying-in Women (1816), and the Dorcas Society for the sick (1826). The Dispensary begun in 1828 was the forerunner of the hospital. As the chapel had its own school, now with 100 boys and 110 girls and an infants' building in Crown Field, the opening of Holy Trinity was followed by that

of the Royal Victoria National School in 1834, to the north of the Calverley Estate. It was designed by Decimus Burton and the Duchess of Kent gave £100 towards its building.[62] Charity for health and basic education was considerable, with royalty helping.

The Coming of a Local Authority

The need for a local authority with compulsory powers to watch, light and drain grew greater. As elsewhere, an association for prosecuting felons was formed in 1816 on account of the weakness of the judicial system. The supply of water was also dealt with by private enterprise. The chalybeate water was considered unfit for normal domestic consumption. In 1814 or 1815 the plumber Thomas Taylor leased a piece of land with a spring some 350 yards south of the Parade from the Earl of Abergavenny. He built a reservoir and pumped water down the hill to the houses on the Parade and on Mount Sion. In 1826 a newly-formed Tunbridge Wells Waterworks Company took over the project. It had 80 shareholders, the shares being worth £50 each and was run by an elected board of directors, consisting of seven members. To ensure an abundant future supply, the company also accepted from the earl a lease of land with a shaft called Water Down Shaft, about 1,500 yards south of the Parade. Taylor was paid £1,000 to erect an engine house and lay pipes from this new property. From the first the company was moderately prosperous. Between 1826 and 1830 the rental varied between £408 5s. to £456 4s. 2d. and dividends from five to seven per cent were paid. In the early 1830s the Calverley Waterworks Company was formed on the Calverley Estate. Besides the estate it supplied houses at the bottom of Mount Pleasant and those adjoining the Common. The water came from a spring near the quarry on the estate, and was pumped from an engine house to a reservoir near Calverley Park.[63]

Since the companies provided adequate water, their rights were protected under the Act that created a local administration in 1835. By the early 1830s there was agitation for a local authority, and in 1832 a committee appointed to consider the advantages of an Act printed its report. It stressed the need for a compulsory rate for watching and lighting. Experience had shown that voluntary arrangements were impracticable, as those with most property were often unwilling to contribute. Several attempts to provide lamp lighting had failed owing to lack of money. A night police was needed, especially to stop the noise and disturbance, and sometimes wanton mischief of people leaving taverns. Also, fly carriages were under no legal control; stands were needed, regulations respecting fares, and some supervision of drivers. This was a matter which particularly concerned a resort where visitors expected to be carried. Again, large drains were wanted, and the power to compel builders to drain into them; much of the town had none, especially the newly-developed Windmill Field and the Lew. 'The practice is to empty slops and refuse of various descriptions into the roads, and the filth is allowed to accumulate by the roadside and in front of houses, not only to the great discomfort of visitors, but to the danger of public health'. Paving was a difficult problem owing to 'the scattered nature of the place'; it was only needed in 'the most frequented thoroughfares', and where the water was not carried off after rain.

In short, the Wells was suffering from the growing pains of a rising town without a local authority to regulate and control its development, and provide amenities and services. Powers were especially needed in a spa. Only a council could furnish the public improvements, which, the report finally stressed, were needed both in the interests of visitors and residents. The prosperity of the Wells had always been, in part, on account of its fine air and healthy surroundings, and there was the implication that its future as a watering space depended on the removal of nuisances and provision of public services.[64]

The final moves began with a general meeting between those paying the poor rate and property owners; it was chaired by Akers and held at the *Royal Sussex Hotel* on 28 October 1833. A committee of 21 leisured people, professional men and prosperous tradespeople was formed to inquire about the cost of obtaining an Act to light and watch the town and regulate the flys; the possible geographical extent of the proposed authority, the rateable value of property within its jurisdiction, and the cost of lighting with gas were issues raised. During the next six weeks these problems were discussed by the committee and a report prepared. But before the committee sought the approval of the general meeting it felt that it needed the consent of the Earl of Abergavenny, the owner of property in the town as well as the largest landowner in the district, of John Ward as owner of the great Calverley Estate, of the Marquess Camden, a landowner on the immediate east of the town, and of Major Gardner as lord of the manor of Rusthall. This was partly to gain financial support in getting the bill through Parliament and partly in recognition of their local influence.

As a result the committee ran into difficulties. It was soon known that Ward feared the interference of the local body in his estate, and wanted it excluded from the bill. Lord Abergavenny also recognised his right to claim exemption. Ward's terms were put to the committee on 27 March 1834. If the bill proceeded in the present parliamentary session he threatened to oppose it at every stage, and was prepared to drain, watch and light his estate at the expense of himself or his tenants. However, if the committee would defer the bill until the next session, would agree to secure the privacy of his estate as far as was consistent with its lighting and watching by the proposed commissioners, and would make two or three other adjustments to the bill, including the acceptance of his right to set up a market on his estate, he would pay half the expenses if his solicitors were associated with those of the townspeople. He also offered £100 towards draining the district round his property. It was not surprising that his wishes prevailed with those of the committee.

Lord Abergavenny's interest had become aroused through his ownership of the waterworks leased by the Tunbridge Wells Waterworks Company. If Ward's undertaking was to be protected in the bill, so must his own. A conference was held in London on 24 April 1835 with Ward and Abergavenny's representative, Lord Nevill. Besides agreeing on their respective undertakings, about 20 alterations to the bill, proposed by the townspeople, were considered. Most of them were accepted at a committee meeting on 27 April and a final draft was prepared.[65]

The bill became an Act of Parliament on 21 July. All owners and occupiers of land worth £50 a year were to be town commissioners. They were given the right to levy rates up to 2s. in the pound, and powers to remove nuisances and rubbish from the streets, appoint watchmen and constables to keep order, construct and repair drains, license carriages and light the town. Special privileges were given to Abergavenny and Ward. Both were allowed to supply water and lay pipes outside their estates. The commissioners were forbidden to convert their private streets into public highways, and Ward was allowed to set up a market on his estate. The whole proceedings, as well as the final bill, revealed the dependence of the town on the local magnates. Their power lay in their extensive urban property and their financial resources, which the townspeople were always tempted to tap for every undertaking involving a large expenditure. As the landowners had directed the planning of the earliest building 150 years before, their influence was paramount in the creation of the new authority.[66]

Part Two:
The Growth of the Modern Town

V   Rapid Expansion: The Second Phase, 1835-1889

The Growth of Society

This period in the history of the town differed from the last in that it had its own secular and ecclesiastical government and many new social institutions. Yet the basic features of the early 19th-century town discussed already, rapid population growth and development as a spa, continued until the 1880s.

The expansion of the town is best shown by simple population figures. Numbers more than doubled between 1821, the earliest year on which one can be certain of the figure, and 1841, rising from 3,934 to 8,302. In the next 50 years population grew three and a half times, the increase being spread evenly over the period: 1841: 8,302; 1851: 10,587; 1861: 13,807; 1871:19,410; 1881: 24,309; 1891: 29,296. Between 1841 and 1901 the town grew as fast as Sevenoaks, Tonbridge and Ashford, all of which were transformed in rather different ways by the coming of the railway. Tunbridge Wells was also helped by the railway. In 1842 the South Eastern Railway Company's line from London via Redhill was opened to Tonbridge, being extended to reach Dover by 1844. Next year a branch line was built as far as the present goods station, to be tunnelled to a station in the town centre in 1846. While the normal coach services had taken huge numbers, such as 31,000 people in 1838, the railway was cheaper and reduced times to London from over four hours to two on most services. Not surprisingly the road traffic declined. The crucial link with the capital was improved by the construction of a more direct line through Sevenoaks and Orpington in 1868. Savidge quotes the 1884 timetable with 20 trains from and 15 trains to Charing Cross on weekdays, taking under one hour. In 1888 the London and Brighton Company offered an alternative route to London via Oxted, only three miles longer than that through Sevenoaks. Meanwhile the town was linked to the coast at Hastings in 1852, and to Brighton in 1866 using another station, the West. Cranbrook, Tenterden and New Romney, either with no rail services or none which were direct, stagnated.

Tunbridge Wells was like other English inland resorts in its rapid growth in the early 19th century. Cheltenham, a sizeable market town, was like it in growing ten times between 1801 and 1851, from 3,076 to 35,051. Leamington rose from a village with 315 people in 1801 to 15,724 in 1851. Clearly the continuation of coach transport was not a hindrance to travel, though it became faster and more comfortable during the period. Then railways increased travel over seven times between 1850 and 1875. While Cheltenham and Leamington did not grow as fast as Tunbridge Wells during the later 19th century, it was surpassed by the rise of the seaside towns of Hastings and Eastbourne, both crucially dependent on the railway.[1]

An explanation of the prosperity of inland and seaside resorts rests partly on the rapid growth of population between 1750 and 1900. In 1750 the population of England and Wales was six or six and a half million; by 1851 it was 17,983,000 and in 1901 32,612,000. Until the 1870s population growth was accompanied by the rising prosperity and living standards of the trading, manufacturing and professional classes. The men enjoyed higher incomes and leisure, passing on money to widows and unmarried daughters. They could all afford travel and holidays. In the last three decades of the 19th century cheap rail journeys and lower food costs made leisure outings possible for most of the working-class population, who were attracted particularly to the seaside. In the whole of the 19th century the upper and middle classes fostered the existing resorts and created new ones.

The importance of the Wells as a resort is shown by the occupations of its inhabitants. The first surviving MS. Census, that of 1841, reveals the pattern of the early Victorian years. Some two-fifths of the whole population, or 3,134 people, worked in a trade or occupation out of whom just over half were labouring men and women. Of these 887, exactly half again, were female servants, and another 245 were male servants. In contrast to this large servant population, there were only some 400 general labourers working in heavy tasks such as building or for brewers or innkeepers, as well as the 140 employed on farms; the rest consisted of 45 gardeners, 82 laundresses, ostlers, porters, 17 coachmen and 10 sempstresses. The local industries were tiny: Tunbridge Ware employed between 23 and 27 people in at least two or three workshops or 'manufactories'; there was also a maker of sweets, a biscuit maker and a soda water maker, again producing luxuries.

There were 275 men in the building trades in addition to labourers, the large number reflecting the rapid expansion of the town; they comprised 10 builders, 111 carpenters and 18 sawyers who presumably included joiners, 33 bricklayers served by eight brickmakers, but only five stonemasons – thus confirming that construction in brick was more important than in stone – and two thatchers; there were also 45 painters, showing the importance of staining and redecorating wood, 13 plasterers for inside and outside work, 14 plumbers and two paperhangers. They were served by an architect, four surveyors and six auctioneers.

Several other occupational groups were largely supported by people of independent means. Three hundred and nineteen were engaged in the clothing and shoemaking trade; as well as the common occupations of tailoring (76 people) and shoemaking (76 men) there were 48 dressmakers, 33 milliners, 52 drapers, six silkmercers, 13 bonnet makers and seven staymakers. By contrast Tonbridge, a typical market town of 3,064 inhabitants, had only four dressmakers, four milliners and 10 drapers. Similarly, the professions were strongly represented at the resort. It had 20 surgeons and physicians helped by 10 chemists, 18 solicitors and one attorney, four bankers, four accountants and 13 clergy, while Tonbridge had five surgeons, four solicitors and an attorney, and three clergy; interestingly although Tonbridge was well represented in schoolmasters on account of the grammar school and in schoolmistresses, the Wells had 11 governesses and five tutors teaching children in prosperous families, with there being only one in Tonbridge; the former town also had five 'professors of music', five artists, a dancing master, a riding master and even a teacher of gymnastics.

Among other occupations dependent on prosperous residents and summer visitors were the 19th-century equivalent of taxi-drivers. While the coachmen were largely employed privately, there were six fly 'proprietors' with 13 'flymen' and six hackneymen. They were much in demand due to the dispersed layout of housing and shops. Those visiting for a few days used the six inns and an hotel, and while 18 lodging housekeepers were noted in the census, many more householders in other occupations offered lodgings in the summer to families staying for at least two or three weeks. Other specialised shopkeepers who sometimes made the goods they sold for moneyed clients included three jewellers, 10 watchmakers, six chairmakers, 15 cabinetmakers, 11 upholsterers; among the food and drink trades in addition to 30 bakers, 48 butchers and 51 grocers were five confectioners, five fishmongers, 12 fruiterers, four poulterers, seven greengrocers, 10 milkmen, nine brewers, two wine merchants and five vintners. The more educated customers used the three stationers, six booksellers, the postmaster, two postmen and eight postboys. The presence of 12 coal merchants confirms that nearly all residents now stayed in the town in winter.

The town also depended for its livelihood on the neighbouring countryside, especially a wide area of north-east Sussex. The 17 blacksmiths, 15 smiths, two farriers, four saddlers and four wheelwrights served the neighbouring farming communities as well as townspeople. The 140 agricultural labourers worked on 15 farms outside the town; corn grown there was bought by five dealers who used six millers. Yet the economy was relatively less dependent on farming than a typical market town; thus Tonbridge, which was less than half the size of the Wells, had 18 blacksmiths, five smiths, five farriers, five wheelwrights and five saddlers.

The most singular feature of its people was the number of adults who did not work. While in Tonbridge there were 60, in the Wells there were 539, mostly belonging to the prosperous leisured class. They were spinster or widowed gentlewomen, retired soldiers, sailors, professional and business men and one or two noblemen and peeresses. It was they who, with the seasonal visitors, provided the town with much of its livelihood.[2]

As one might expect at a spa, this social pattern continued during the following decades. In 1851, according to Savidge, 13.4 per cent of the whole population were servants, more than twice the national average at a time when domestic service was the most numerous occupation after farming. Women outnumbered men chiefly because of the relative shortage of work for them in the Sussex and Kent countryside, while in the Wells women were needed as maids and general servants in prosperous households, and in the clothing trades such as dressmaking, millinery and drapery. Bath and the other resorts had a similar predominance of females.[3]

The occupations of people on the Parade in 1871 show both the trades typical of all towns and those more prominent in resorts. The status of the working population which totalled 264 is often mentioned. Of the 36 drapers, 10 were described as 'drapers' (of whom four were probably assistants), two as linen and woollen drapers, 21 as draper's assistants and three as apprentices. There was a master tailor employing 16 men and boys, with five tailors, a tailor's assistant and an apprentice who may have all been working for the master tailor, some at least at home. The shop assistants were plentiful in the food and drink trades; with two grocer and wine merchants and a grocer were 13 grocer's assistants. The baker and confectioner had two shop assistants. Makers and retailers of luxury goods included a jeweller, working jeweller and an apprentice. There were two china merchants named Luck, a widow and her son in partnership, the occupant of a toy bazaar with an assistant, and another with a 'berlin and fancy repository'. Photography was now represented by an artist photographer and an assistant. With a printer were six men in bookselling, including two assistants and an apprentice and a 'manager' with a clerk. To provide entertainment were two musicians and a seller of music and other goods. Professional men included a surgeon and a physician served by a master dispensing chemist, a chemist's assistant and an apprentice. Prosperous people could hire the professor for pianoforte and singing and six governesses for their children. Eighty-two or nearly one-third of the working inhabitants were servants, including 23 maids, 10 cooks, 14 'domestic' and 12 'general' servants, all well distributed among the shopkeepers as well as being especially represented in the *Sussex* and *Swan* hotels. The 14 people of independent means, retired or of no occupation included two former army and two naval officers.

The households to the west and north of the Common, which had 230 working occupants, included two solicitors, an attorney, four clergy and two music teachers among the professional people, with three engineers, two coach builders, two fly proprietors, three lodging housekeepers and a manufacturer of Tunbridge Ware. Yet those people not working and their male and female servants greatly predominated, especially in the large houses of Hungershall Park and Nevill Park; there were 28 of the former and 157 of the latter. Thus at no. 5 Nevill Park lived an 'annuitant', James Walker aged 69, his wife, four daughters in their twenties who were not working, and a visitor; the typical domestic staff comprised a cook, two housemaids, a kitchen maid and a butler.[4]

In 1886, when the population was probably 26,000 or 27,000 George Stevens's *Directory of Tunbridge Wells, Tonbridge and Neighbourhood* lists just under 2,000 men and women according to their occupation; they comprised retailers, master craftsmen, manufacturers and professional men and women; assistants, apprentices and other trainees were normally excluded. Officials of the Local Board, government officials and bankers were noted elsewhere. Innumerable visitors stayed at the 17 hotels and the 212 lodging houses now sometimes called apartments and boarding houses, which also presumably had semi-permanent residents. Both visitors and the more prosperous townspeople hired the services of nine bath chair proprietors, 25 fly and carriage proprietors, and 13 job masters and livery stable keepers to move among the much dispersed housing and public buildings of the town, and to visit country houses and other rural attractions; all these people needed, periodically, to buy from the eight coach and carriage builders, which included the carriage works of George Smith in Calverley Road from 1848, who made a variety of wheeled vehicles. There were now 24 booksellers and stationers, some of whom were among the seven bookbinders. Among makers and retailers of luxury goods with a ready sale were four antique dealers, two male and three female managers of Berlin wool and fancy warehouses, 13 china, glass and earthenware dealers, four mineral water and three Tunbridge-Ware manufacturers, seven pictureframe makers, 16 silversmiths and jewellers, four umbrella makers and 12 nurserymen, seedsmen and florists. There were 97 milliners and dressmakers, of whom 75 were naturally female. Teaching both adolescents and adults were four French teachers and 13 teachers and 'professors' of music, the latter being served by six occupants of pianoforte and music warehouses and piano tuners. New occupations included nine photographers by this time, eight gas and hot water fitters and engineers, and five bicycle and tricycle makers, repairers and agents. Among noted photographers was Henry Peach Robinson whose large pictures told a story, mostly country scenes, and Thomas Sims from 1868 who adopted improved processes. Alfred Romary had begun making wafer-thin biscuits in Church Road in 1862. The most notable artist was the elder C.T. Dodd (1815-78) of Grosvenor Lodge who taught at Tonbridge School and showed at the Royal Academy.

The majority of the professional men, shopkeepers, craftsmen and labourers and their wives were born locally. The numerous Delves family descended from Richard Delves (1727-1804), who was born in Waldron, Sussex and moved to the town, as already mentioned. Three of his descendants had a butcher's shop in Chapel Place, one was a grocer, one a steward to the

Abergavenny Estate, and another, William Henry (1829-1922), was secretary to the Walks Estate, chairman of a building society and a town commissioner in 1882. Descendants of the attorney Stone included Frank William, twice Mayor. In 1871 the gardener in the stables of no. 11 Hungershall Park, Edward Edwards, aged 31, came from Hartfield, his wife from Frant and the four children had been born locally. By contrast Francis Lamping, 'head draper' at nos. 8-10 the Parade, came from Devon to work in the town, no doubt being attracted by the fashion trade. Nearly all the people of independent means were not of local origin, but came from London, its suburbs in Middlesex and Surrey, the Midlands, the North and even Scotland. An example of the residents of Nevill and Hungershall Parks in 1871 can be seen at no. 5 Hungershall Park where lived Richard Deakin, aged 62, a doctor no longer practising; his wife came from Derby, the cook from Sussex and the housemaid from Kent. In Park Road in 1891 there were many householders of independent means, about half of whom were widows; while hardly any were born in the town, some came from London and Surrey. The leisured inhabitants and working population differed in geographical origin as well as social standing.[5]

The Spread of Houses and Public Buildings

The rapid growth of population in the mid-19th century led to the building of much of the modern town. There was a huge extension of its boundaries. The characteristics of a resort continued, with many substantial houses in large gardens and sometimes adjoining parks. The building of the Calverley Estate was practically finished by the end of the 1830s. Yet, as already mentioned, the market hall proved abortive as a market site, becoming the Town Hall instead. The Promenade, a crescent of 17 shops with lodgings

48 *View of Nevill Park across the valley from Hungershall Park; the space between them was left vacant to provide uninterrupted views from both rows of houses.*

above, which included at the start baths, a shop selling Tunbridge Ware and fancy goods, a library and a 'bazaar' soon became purely residential. For at least three decades the Parade remained the only trading centre.

As a residential suburb the Calverley Estate was a rapid success, taking 11 or 12 years to complete. It seemed to have met a pent-up demand for substantial, architecturally-designed houses in an organised park-like setting. Villas were fashionable in the 1830s as well as terraced houses in a crescent. They were mostly erected before the national slump in building for five or six years from 1837. It probably affected two or three similarly spacious projects with far fewer large houses. On the west of the Common 10 detached villas called Nevill Park, erected on a building lease from the Abergavenny Estate from 1831, were to cost at least £1,000; four were built by 1838; then after a pause the other six appeared between 1847 and 1863; an eleventh costing £2,132 and set in 50 acres, was added at one end. Also on the estate, across a valley to be left open, 11 similar houses were built as Hungershall Park between 1854 and 1867. To some extent they were in competition with properties erected in the 1850s and 1860s along the Frant Road and Broadwater Down also on Abergavenny land. Five large houses, each on an acre sold by Marquess Camden in Camden Park to the east of the Calverley Estate with seven-and-a-half acres of open land, were built in the 1850s and 1860s. Progress was slow, with expensive plots along Bayhall Road not being sold until about 1875 and houses being built in the following years in contemporary Norman Shaw style. On the north-west of the Common, Bishops Down Park on the estate of Colonel Weller, lord of the manor of Rusthall, was largely abortive: in 1864 and 1865 31 lots were sold in a circular road round a lake, but only four houses, one being huge, were built. Clearly demand for such properties was limited both by the capital cost and the need to fill them with five or six servants. In the 1850s and 1860s other large houses costing perhaps between £1,000 and £2,000 were built along Sandrock, Lansdowne and Pembury Roads in piecemeal developments. In the 1870s and 1880s Ferndale Park was created with 40 houses, again on large plots, by 1886. The slow development of such estates is well illustrated by the case of Sandown Park, where six houses were built in about 20 years from 1869 on a private gated road

49 *Two of the substantial houses in Nevill Park erected on building leases from the Abergavenny Estate in the mid-19th century.*

with an entrance lodge, and some with their own lodge; among others noted for their architecture, Pembury Grange was designed by the celebrated George Devey.

Yet part of the northern extension of the town comprised four-roomed two-storey cottages costing only £50 or £60 for skilled and unskilled workers. While one or two developments of such tenements consisted of a group of streets such as that on the Windmill Field in the 1830s, others consisted of a street or part of a street such as those built later in Quarry Road and Goods Station Road. Medium-sized houses for the middle classes in the mid-19th century were in terraces of two or three storey with basements, or were semi-detached and detached dwellings. They had six or eight mostly large, tall rooms, including a kitchen, drawing room, dining room, three or four bedrooms and attics, costing £200 or £300 and upwards. Such houses were built in Hydraulic (now Beulah Road) in the 1850s; by 1867 there were 27 in St James' Road, and there was similar building along Camden Road. To the west, near the London Road, the Conservative Land Society bought 60 acres in 1856; they sold 75 lots for £7,667 6s., which is an average of about £102 each, between the new Queens and Upper Grosvenor Roads, and in 1863, the final 37 lots at £63 to £77, the buyers pledging support for the Party. The society paid for the roads and drainage across the estate. It went on buying land; in August 1861 it made the 45th purchase, by St John's Church and adjoining Woodbury Park Road, when land prices were said to have quadrupled in the last 10 years. Building was still

50 *No. 2 Hungershall Park showing the mouldings above the windows.*

51 *Landsdowne Road in the 1860s; the houses are substantial and semi-detached in a wide road.*

52 *Earl's Court built in 1866 by the Hon. F.G. Molyneux where he lived until his death in 1886; afterwards three storeys were added for a hotel; from the 1950s it was occupied by Reliant Insurance.*

53 Wellington Hotel, *built on Mount Ephraim in 1875; a massive building taking full advantage of its position overlooking the Common and the town centre beyond it.*

incomplete by 1889. Houses, including some in the Gothic style, were built in the neighbouring Woodbury Park and Park Roads in the later 1870s and 1880s; they were tree-lined without parks.

Meanwhile rebuilding and improvement to existing houses took place and new houses and shops in the older parts of the town were built. Some of the houses with shops on the Parade were rebuilt in the mid-19th century. Many of the houses in the High Street and in the adjoining short Castle Street, Chapel Place and Nevill Street were built or rebuilt with shops. On Mount Sion hill there was rebuilding and infilling with private dwellings and lodging houses. In the 1870s shops with two storeys above were built up the east side of Mount Pleasant and along the south side of Calverley Road. The biggest shops were Weekes and Paine's 'drapery store' on the corner of Mount Pleasant and Grove Hill Road, and Waymark 'drapers' suppliers' at the corner of Calverley and Mount Pleasant Roads, begun by Ebenezer Waymark in 1876. To the early 19th-century Grove Hill Gardens was added Grove Hill Road with houses dated about 1860, and mid-19th-century houses in Claremont Road. Building took place along the main northbound Grosvenor Road, the streets to its south towards Church Road, in London Road and Mount Ephraim.[6]

House building was accompanied by a varied range of new or adapted public buildings. Among the most important hotels which were new or rebuilt, the *Wellington* on Mount Ephraim with its fine views was built in 1875, and the *Royal Kentish* at the back of the Parade was enlarged in 1878. *Bishops Down Spa* was a huge hotel for health treatment built in 1878 and run by a Hydropathic Sanatorium Company. The Dispensary which started in 1828 became the Infirmary in a substantial building in Grosvenor Road in 1842, and the still larger General Hospital in 1884; it continued to be voluntarily supported. Four buildings for various cultural activities appeared in the 1870s. The largest was the Great Hall at the foot of Mount Pleasant designed by the local architect H.H. Cronk in contemporary French style, with a large hall and club rooms above, which cost a company of shareholders over £13,000. Two years later the Mechanics Institute occupied special premises in Dudley Road; it was in yellow brick with red brick bands and financed by Hon F.G. Molyneux and T.E. Gibson among many subscribers. The Pump Room of 1878 at the end of the Parade with a hall, library, reading and club rooms for the more prosperous was built by a company to rival the Great Hall. The brick Friendly Societies Hall was intended for popular meetings. The Corn Exchange had replaced the theatre on the Parade. The elementary schools for boys, girls and infants naturally had new buildings.[7]

It was the great age of church and chapel building. Apart from the neo-Norman white brick and stone Christ Church in the High Street built for £8,500 by its minister in 1835-41, and the chancel added to King Charles Church in 1887, the Anglican churches ringed the suburbs in roads where house building was under way, and which they encouraged. The original St John in St John's Road was built in 1858 for £3,044, closely followed by the larger St James in Sandrock Road in 1860-2 at £6,000, the fabric being given by the Ward family. Like them St Peter, in Bayhall Road towards the east, was designed in the medieval decorated style in 1874-5. In the southern outskirts the Earl of Abergavenny, a clergyman, paid for St Mark in Broadwater Down to be built in an Italian Gothic style in 1864-6. Finally in 1870 a mission church called St Stephen was built in Stanley Road to attract poorer people; it was replaced by the large St Barnabas in 1888, costing £18,000. Fourteen or fifteen non-Anglican church buildings of varying sizes were the result of donations and pew rents. Among them was the classical Roman Catholic St Augustine in Grosvenor Road of 1837-8, the Congregational chapel on Mount Pleasant of 1845-8 costing £3,700, to which the portico was added in 1866 for £1,400, the Emmanuel on Mount Ephraim built by the Countess of Huntingdon's Connexion in 1867 for £5,000, the Wesleyan chapel in Vale Road costing £5,000 in 1872-3, and the Baptist Tabernacle in Calverley Road of 1883 built for £5,759. In size and design they competed with the Anglican churches.[8]

From the 1830s until his death in 1875, William Willicombe with his partner William Oakley dominated the house building trade, working almost everywhere from the Parade and the High Street to Pembury and Sandrock Roads; they also erected the Wesleyan chapel in Vale Road and St Peter, Bayhall Road. Among later builders were Edwards Bros in Woodbury Park Road, where they had a yard, after 1877 and J.S. Weare who was responsible

54 *Christ Church, built 1836-41 in a neo-Norman style and paid for by its first minister.*

55 *St Mark in Broadwater Down, built in 1864-6 in a late Italian Gothic style. It was paid for by the Revd Wm, 4th Earl of Abergavenny.*

56 *St James in Sandrock Road, built in 1860-2 with a north aisle added in 1880; the original fabric was given by the Ward family of the Calverley Estate and designed by Ewan Christian.*

for Ferndale and started the High Brooms Brick and Tile Company in 1885. Acting as an intermediary between landowner and builder was profitable. The leading property developer was Charles Adie; originally a solicitor's clerk he become a brickmaker, auctioneer and builder, who acquired land to have houses and shops erected on Mount Pleasant and in Calverley Road, as well as houses in Woodbury Park Road and its neighbourhood. Although he went bankrupt in 1877, he left an extraordinary physical mark.[9]

Religion, Schooling, and Culture

The interests and outlook of the large resident leisured class supported by many professional and well-to-do tradesmen and even the visitors, helped to shape the new and developing institutions. The encouragement of luxury products, including articles of fashionable clothing has already been mentioned. As churchgoing was normal among the middle classes, whether Anglican or Nonconformist, one would expect a strong attendance in the town, with the numerous carriages, which were owned or hired, being much used on each occasion. Attention is always paid to the unique religious census of 1851, though there was no return for Holy Trinity. The Baptists, Congregationalists, Methodists and adherents of the Countess of Huntingdon's Connexion were all strongly represented. With its 1,427 sittings and most probably three services, total attendance will have been much higher at Holy Trinity than at any other church. Anglican attendance in the town will have been greater than Nonconformist. In general the religious pattern was conservative as there were no Primitive Methodists and the middle-class congregation of the Connexion was quasi-Anglican. Total attendance will have been much larger in proportion to the whole population than the proportion in Kent as a whole.[10]

THE RELIGIOUS CENSUS OF 1851

	Morning	Afternoon	Evening
Christ Church	500	120	450
King Charles Church	c.800	c.300	
St Augustine, Roman Catholic	130	70	
Mount Sion, Congregational	50		
Baptist, Grosvenor Road	120	20	120
Wesleyan, Hanover Road	550	300	
Congregational, Mount Pleasant	392	275	
Baptist, Hanover Road	295	190	180
Countess of Huntingdon's Connexion	301	220	

57 *St Peter in Bayhall Road, adjoining Windmill Fields; it was designed by H.H. Cronk and built by Willicombe and Oakley in 1874-5, with a north aisle in 1889.*

More striking is a sample by the Vicar of Holy Trinity in 1860 of 200 families in his parish which showed only 142 (35 per cent) 'whose habit is to live without the public worship of God', a particularly high figure when the sick, disabled and Sunday working people are considered. Missions included those to the outlying tenements of Tutty's Village in Frant parish, where a small chapel was erected in 1839, and that in a church called St Stephen built in 1870 in Stanley Road off Camden Road, again intended for working men and women. In the 1880s the Salvation Army arrived with its clamorous parades and the inevitable accompanying disturbances. In 1885 two visitors, the Misses Wells, bought the old gasworks site in Varney Street, a poor area off Calverley Road for the building of a headquarters.[11]

The clergy and missioners rose to the demand. There were several notable men in religious and social life among the clergy. Most prominent was Edward Hoare, Vicar of Holy Trinity from 1853 till his death in 1894. Coming from a banking family, he had served previously in Ramsgate, a seaside resort with a similar leisured class. A Protestant Evangelical, his strong voice filled Holy Trinity with clear, sincere sermons where his congregation was said to be over 1,600; his Sunday services ended with a mission service in the parish room for about 300 'poorer and labouring people' who were not regular churchgoers; there were five Sunday schools and many classes for 'all sorts and conditions of men' and women. He often spoke to religious bodies elsewhere including London. He was on numerous town committees and spoke at public gatherings, his sermons and addresses reaching a wide public through the local newspapers. The statue erected in his memory in St John's Road marked the extraordinary influence his strong religious character had had in the town. The Rev. W.L. Pope who was at King Charles Church for 50 years (1829-79) was interested in schools and helping the poor and contributed to the work of local institutions, such as the Infirmary. On one occasion, at a public meeting in 1858, he proposed using the unemployed to create a lake for children; once completed it was known popularly as 'Pope's puddles' (later Brighton Lake).[12]

Like the other leading watering-places of Bath and Cheltenham, the Wells was a centre of Evangelicalism. Yet disputes over the liturgy arose on account of ritualist practices introduced by the Vicar of St James, C.R. Pearson, and the clergy of St Stephen (which became St Barnabas in 1888 under the patronage of Keble College) appointing 'high churchmen' as a Tractarian foundation. Such practices as the wearing of a surplice by the clergy in services, bowings, incense and candles horrified

58 *View of the interior of St Barnabas Church, Stanley Road, 1889-90; the only 'High Church'.*

devout churchgoers and seemed to be Roman Catholic. The local Evangelical clergy were so opposed that they offered to enlarge the accommodation of existing churches as an alternative to the building of St Barnabas. Controversy also split the Baptists when Thomas Edwards, a fine preacher and composer of a hymn-book, was minister of Rehoboth in Chapel Place. In 1866 he renounced adult believers' baptism, and part of his congregation built him Salem in St John's Road. From 1852 Thomas Jay of the Town Mission and Ragged Schools Society ran a mission in a building in Golding Street, a poor district, which was partly a school and partly a centre for preaching to and rehabilitating young men and women who had fallen into bad ways. Attached to all the Anglican churches were elementary schools, usually for boys, girls and infants. By far the oldest was that at King Charles Church, said to date almost from its foundation. The Boys School was now in a building in Chapel Place; in the 1880s with room for 200 boys it had a reputation under its headmaster W.A. Diggens as an 'excellent school'; from 1858 the Girls and Infants School, which also benefited from Pope's keen interest, was in Murray House on Mount Sion. Numbers at each elementary school in the 1880s ran from under one hundred to nearly three hundred. The St James's Schools in Quarry Road comprised a boys school for 250 under a headmaster and three assistant masters, a girls school for 129 with a headmistress and two assistant mistresses, and an infants school for 195 with a headmistress and three assistant mistresses. By this time there was a Higher Grade School for 200 boys and a Middle Grade School for girls, the latter being started by the minister of Emmanuel Church, George Jones, with the help of a wealthy benefactor; such schools were appearing in larger towns for children of thirteen or fourteen. Lastly, in 1887 the Skinners' Company founded the Skinners School to give a largely commercial secondary education, due to pressure from Molyneux and other inhabitants. Fifty-three boys were enrolled at first; in fact the classics were as important as at public schools, perhaps because of the wishes of some parents.[13]

The clergy helped to run the local branches of the leading English missionary societies such as the Society for the Propagation of Christian Knowledge and the British and Foreign Bible Society; from time to time senior ministers addressed fund-raising meetings. They also encouraged societies fostering reading, discussion and study of religious, moral and other issues; in the 1880s they included the Emmanuel Branch of the Young Men's Mutual Improvement Society and among large temperance groups attached to churches, the St James' Branch of the Church of England Temperance Society.

With so many prosperous families, small private schools proliferated, their number reaching 25 by 1886: 14 were for 'ladies', eight for 'gentlemen' and three 'preparatory', mostly being run by one or two teachers; presumably some older local boys were

59 *The Skinners School, St John's Road, 1887: a grammar school intended for boys destined for business and trade, founded by the Skinners' Company with local encouragement.*

sent to public schools including Tonbridge. While some schools lasted no longer than the working life of the teachers, others such as Rose Hill, a preparatory school dating from the 1860s, became permanent institutions. Adult education grew in the mid-19th century. From 1872 the Mechanics Institute in its new premises had library, reading and lecture rooms; there were art and science classes with students being described as 'ladies', 'middle class' and 'artisans'. In the 1880s there were Sunday 'adult classes for working men' in the Friendly Societies Hall; thus the labouring classes were not ignored.

Public entertainments were changing and becoming more varied. The theatre on the Parade finally closed in 1843 after several seasons of plays were unsuccessful; the local decline of interest in drama was part of a national trend. The Great Hall from 1870 was the only building licensed for drama but it was mainly used for concerts, lectures and meetings. Prominent in cultural activities was the Literary Society founded in 1836, which met on the Parade; used by visitors as well as residents, it had a growing library and reading room which opened daily. The existence of a

Choral Society in 1862, and a permanent Vocal Society from 1870, showed the popularity of music and the extent to which people were prepared to sing together. The Amateur Photographic Association began in 1887. The Tunbridge Wells Bonfire and Recreation Society met weekly in the 1880s for discussion and liquid refreshment at the *Railway Bell Hotel*, and held concerts at various places. By this time there was an Ornithological Society, and a Natural History Society with a collection for study. The Chrysanthemum, Horticultural (dating from 1836) and Pen societies held shows so that their activities became widely known. The Tunbridge Wells Society for Protection against Cruelty to Animals had patrons, a committee of 26, and honorary and paid staff, thus showing the importance attached to the proper care of horses used in transport and on farms, and the suitable treatment of pets.

60 *Terraced artisans' dwellings of four or five rooms in Rusthall, of the mid-19th century.*

Reading and discussion of matters of local and general interest were encouraged in other ways. Clubs based on the London model appeared by the 1870s; the Tunbridge Wells Club started in 1872 occupying the first floor of the Great Hall with its library, reading room, refreshment and games rooms. After the opening of the Pump Room the Nevill Club met there with similar facilities. While these clubs were intended for leisured and professional men, tradesmen and artisans were served at the same time by a Working Men's Club and a Church of England Working Men's Society each with rooms in the north of the town. Among societies with a specific interest or interests were the Tradesmen's Association started in 1858 and the Association for Promoting the Interests of the Town from 1874. The clubs with political aims which appeared by the 1880s were predominantly Conservative, although the Liberal Party was also represented. With the Corn Exchange, which replaced the theatre, the Wells was a considerable market centre. It was reflected in the Tunbridge Wells Agricultural Association which ran a celebrated annual August show from 1862; the Farmers Club founded in 1870 met to read papers and discuss matters of agricultural concern. As one might expect in most sizeable towns, there were two well-established masons' lodges and many friendly societies. With numerous visitors, leisured residents and prosperous professional men and tradesmen, newspapers flourished from the 1850s. The *Gazette* began in 1853, there were several papers in the 1860s and those beginning later included *The Kent and Sussex Courier* from 1872 and *The Kent and Sussex Advertiser* from 1881.[14]

Among sports, cricket was becoming increasingly popular. There was an upper and a lower ground on the Common, Kent playing on the former between 1845 and the 1880s. The founding of the Blue Mantles Club with well-to-do patronage in 1862 was followed by the start of two or three other clubs in the 1870s and 1880s. In 1885-6 the lower ground was enlarged, levelled and railed in by unemployed workmen. By this time football, cycling and swimming (with an open air bath at the end of Quarry Road) were all organised; hunting with two packs was also available. For most of the 19th century three generations of the Cramp family had a fashionable riding establishment with a riding school and Bath House in Grosvenor Road.

The pursuit of health continued to be a main attraction for visitors and leisured residents. Drinking the chalybeate waters stayed fashionable. Subscribers paid for a portico over the spring in 1847, on completion of which new rules for the attendance of dippers, their charges and overall cleanliness on the advice of local doctors were adopted. Later the Pump Room provided a rival with its own spring for drinking. Bathing grew in popularity as an invigorating and health-giving activity. There were several private baths. In 1847 no. 1 Calverley Promenade was occupied by Mrs Sarah Thomas who offered 'warm, shower and medicated baths'. Hydropathy on the grand scale was provided from 1878 by *Bishops Down Spa* where Turkish and other bathing was offered on the advice of a doctor for many thousands of people each year, many of whom used the innumerable hotel rooms and strolled and sat in the extensive grounds with their wonderful views. Such baths were the great attraction of English and foreign spas.

The high proportion of prosperous people meant that charities were amply supported. The dispensaries and hospitals were entirely supported by voluntary contributions in the form of large donations, regular subscriptions and street and even church collections. Besides the General Hospital, there was a Homeopathic Hospital from 1863 and an Eye and Ear Hospital from 1878. There was growing help for the unemployed and hungry. While beggars were everywhere it is likely that they were especially attracted to the town by its numerous wealthy households. The Mendicity Society was presided over by F.G. Molyneux, son of the Earl of Sefton and a leading townsman who lived in a mansion on Mount Ephraim, and by 1886 it had a committee of 11 including two clergymen and a part-time paid official. The soup kitchens attached to several churches were much needed in cold winters and times of heavy unemployment. Food and coal were sometimes paid for cheaply by ticket, sometimes free. A bread and milk fund begun in 1848 became permanent; based on voluntary subscriptions it helped the poor in winter and the sick, with milk and rolls paid for by cheap tickets. By the 1880s there were several charitable homes for women and children. They included the Orphans' Home for Destitute Children in St John's Road (with another building in Southwark) for girls between four and sixteen. Several wealthy people and families supported most good causes, often with large sums. In addition to the clergy who financed new churches and Molyneux there was T. Jones-Gibb who had made money in the East, paid for the spire of St Peter's, and gave generously to the hospital and the Middle Grade School for Girls of 1882.[15]

Administrative Changes

The Town Commission lasted throughout the period, becoming a Local Board of Health from 1860. It met on the first Monday of each month in the Town Hall after the first years. At the first meeting on 27 July 1835 under the chairmanship of John Stone, 95 propertied people qualified as commissioners, with 30 more qualifying on 3 August. Numbers present varied sharply over the years, with insufficient attendance on many occasions, and a large figure when matters were of great interest. Thus 37 appeared under the chairmanship of William Delves in January 1860 when the tolls of the Wadhurst and Tunbridge Wells Turnpike Trust were being discussed. The terms of the 1835 Act were strengthened in 1846. In 1860 the elective clauses of the 1858 Local Government Act were adopted. Men and women owning or occupying property worth £30 a year elected 24 commissioners for a three-year term, with plural voting for those with higher incomes. From the 1850s its committees included police, paving and drainage, rating and finance, and others for more temporary purposes. The leisured inhabitants were strongly represented. F.G. Molyneux was chairman for 16 years. In 1867/8 among the other 23 members were two retired naval captains and probably eight others of independent means. The other commissioners were prominent tradespeople and professional men. At this date there were two surgeons, a solicitor, an auctioneer, surveyor and a bookseller.[16]

The original officials were a town clerk, surveyor, rate collector and police superintendent. It expanded especially in the last 20 or 25 years as the town's needs grew and local government laws increased. In 1835 a superintendent and five constables in uniform were appointed. By 1847 there was a superintendent, sergeant and eight men, with an office from then on at the

Because of Tunbridge Wells' importance as a fashionable resort, its elevation to borough status attracted national publicity. The Illustrated London News sent an artist to record this scene at the Town Hall with William Cripps (also top right) reading the charter and a top-hatted Mayor Stone-Wigg (inset left) standing behind

Beginning of the borough

FORTY YEARS ago in February, 1952, the death of William Charles Cripps at the age of 97 ended a direct link with Victorian times. For he was the first Town Clerk of Tunbridge Wells and main organiser of the triumphant return from London with the Borough Charter in 1889.

The name of Cripps, a solicitor in private practice and part-time Clerk to the Local Board before 1889, lives on in the Tunbridge Wells law firm of Cripps, Harries, Hall.

From his office it was just a step across Calverley Road to the Town Hall opposite. Never successful as the market for which it was designed, this Town Hall served Tunbridge Wells until the new civic centre opened just before the last war.

Before 1889, the town's affairs were supervised by a Local Board of 24 "improvement commissioners" responsible under two Acts of Parliament for developing local facilities and amenities.

Stone-Wigg called an urgent meeting of his Local Board and the decision was quickly taken to petition the Privy Council for a charter.

After a period of anxious waiting, the town's new status was approved and on February 27, 1889, William Cripps and 20 others - some chosen by ballot to avoid argument travelled to London to collect the precious parchment and returned in special coaches attached to the Hastings train.

The townspeople's previous in-difference had been transformed. Fog signals placed on the line exploded in welcome as the train neared Tunbridge Wells. In the freezing wind and blowing snow, outside the station waited a vast procession led by the Yeomanry and Volunteers with their bands and including contingents from every local organisation.

Cripps and Stone-Wigg led the parade in a four-horse carriage waving the charter in its red and

gold case. Jubilant crowds cheered them all the way to the flag-bedecked Town Hall, where the Charter of Incorporation was read.

Three hundred worthies sat down to an elaborate lunch in the Great Hall at the foot of Mount Pleasant. The only complaint was that the hall's notoriously poor acoustics made it difficult to hear the speeches. That evening the whole town celebrated with a fire-work "salute of 21 guns".

Charter Day was marked permanently with the planting of a group of lime trees at the junction of Major Yorke's Road and Hungershall Park.

John Stone-Wigg was the Charter Mayor. William Cripps served the borough as Town Clerk until his retirement in 1925, when he was made a Freeman of the Borough. Four years later he was elected a member of Kent County Council.

61   On 27 February 1889, Tunbridge Wells received the charter creating it a borough. The picture shows the Town Clerk, William Cripps (insert right), reading it and the chairman of the Local Board, J. Stone-Wigg (insert left) standing behind in the top hat.

Town Hall. By 1886 they comprised a superintendent, five sergeants and 25 constables. At first the police were involved with presenting nuisances which could be removed under the terms of the Act; these included signboards overhanging footpaths and doors opening onto them. In the catching of petty criminals they seem to have been relatively efficient; in 1859 out of 43 larcenies the perpetrators were caught in 15 cases; in 1860 figures were much better with 26 out of 32 larcenies being resolved. From 1835 tenders were received for annual scavenging contracts. Firefighting was given much attention and behind the Town Hall was a house for the fire engine. In 1847 there was a director and nine men on call. By 1886 the service had two part-time directors and 16 men with a manual engine, and a larger volunteer fire brigade supported by subscriptions. By 1886 officials included a town clerk and his assistant, treasurer, collector of rates, surveyor and waterworks engineer, two inspectors of nuisances who were in effect sanitary officers, an inspector of petroleum and explosives (presumably a relatively new officer) and a medical officer of health (a compulsory official from 1872). On account of its size and regional importance several public officers worked in the town, including a registrar of births, marriages and deaths, an inspector of weights and measures and government tax officials.[17]

Water continued to be provided privately for the first 30 years. The newer northern part of the town was now able to draw piped water from the Calverley Waterworks reservoir fed by Jack's Spring. Yet many dwellings had their own wells. In 1865 the Board bought out the two companies, building its own reservoir in Pembury. However, supply became increasingly inadequate over the next 20 years, especially in dry summers when roads were watered. Naturally the potential cost of improvement was the hindrance. Finally £33,000 was spent between 1881 and 1885 on a new scheme which was dogged by problems including the failure of contractors to complete. It involved a seven-acre reservoir in Pembury, valve and pumping engine houses, and a rising main two miles long to the Blackhurst reservoir east of the town. Paving and drainage received constant attention from the commissioners. Thus on 6 January 1860 the Rating and Finance Committee received estimates; the Police Committee needed £542, the Paving and Drainage Committee £770 and the committee itself £145, totalling £1,457, to be raised by a 6d. rate for six months from February; there was a separate estimate for paving to cost £962 from a 3d. rate. Expenditure had risen several times since the commission began work. When the Act was sought, an annual expenditure of about £1,200 was planned, and in August 1835 the commission borrowed £1,200 at five per cent from the local bankers, Messrs Beeching, to pay charges before the first rates were levied. It did not pay for gas, which as usual in English towns was privately supplied. A partnership (Messrs Berry) provided gas lighting until 1843, after which it came from a company. The Police and Lighting Committee placed the first 111 lamps with suitable burners and lanterns in 1836, the rate collector paying two lamplighters 15s. a week. From the first there were bye-laws governing carriages plying for hire, including their fares and standings, 39 carriages being licensed in 1835.[18]

Because of its role as a spa, health in the town was particularly important. There was an extraordinary episode in 1864 when a new resident, Dr Webber of no. 1 Sion Terrace, complained in a letter to the Home Office that a drain in the London Road was insanitary and was causing illness; while its inspector after a careful investigation denied the allegations, local tradesmen were furious about the damage to the reputation of the town. A huge mob caused a riot outside his house, throwing stones to break the windows. In 1868 a sewage scheme was planned, and two sewage farms to the north and south of the town were created in the early 1870s.[19]

A succession of ecclesiastical parishes was created, based on the new churches, beginning with Holy Trinity in 1833, followed by Christ Church (1856), St John's (1859), St James (1862), St Peter's (1876), St Barnabas (1881) and King Charles the Martyr (1889). Civil administrative changes were fiercely debated in the 1880s. In 1881 equal voting by ballot for all ratepayers and incorporation as a borough was urged by the Tradesmen's Association. The reformers formed the Incorporation League, and for eight years there were meetings, pamphlets, petitions and newspaper comment in favour. However, the majority on the Board defended their work as sound, claiming that change would involve higher rates; plural voting by the conservative-minded stopped the reformers when they stood for election. Almost 200 people including the printer Richard Pelton signed a declaration of dissent against reform. Then in 1888 the chairman, Stone-Wigg, realised that the new Local Government Act establishing county councils made advantageous the acquisition of borough status. The Board petitioned for a charter, which was delivered in January 1889. The town now had a mayor, a council of 24 with a three-year term and six aldermen appointed by the Council for six years. Four wards elected six councillors each, with a total of 3,594 burgesses initially with one vote, plural voting having been abolished.

Its authority was almost immediately extended and consolidated. By the Improvement Act of 1890 the Council took over the Grove and assumed partial control of the Common. It issued corporation stock worth £126,000 and its responsibilities for water supply, the regulation of new buildings and streets and other public health matters were defined. In 1893 the borough was granted its own quarter sessions. As tradesmen and craftsmen were J.Ps as well as leisured and professional men, the upper and middle classes were broadly represented. Independence was completed with the creation of Tunbridge Wells and Broadwater Down civil parishes, thus paying their own poor rates; it meant final separation from the parishes of Tonbridge, Speldhurst and Frant.[20]

VI Further Change, 1889-1939

The Years of Growth

The rapid growth of the population was ending by the 1890s and 1900s, and it was stationary between 1911 and 1931. The figures were 29,296 (1891), 33,373 (2001), 35,568 (1911) and 35,367 (1931). Yet the unusual social pattern continued in the early 20th century, with a disproportionate number of leisured residents and a majority of women, some of whom worked in service for the prosperous minority. There seem to have been more visitors than before, and by the 1920s and 1930s men and women working in London were becoming numerous. While there were probably slightly fewer retired people, the middle-aged and elderly were still unusually numerous. Manufacturing remained on too small a scale to provide much alternative work.

The transformation in local government in 1889-90 ushered in a decade or more of wide-ranging improvement. It was partly, perhaps largely, through the Council that public amenities were developed and greatly extended. The continued immigration of the 1890s and early 1900s added to the need for housing, public building and a widening range of cultural and sporting entertainments. Yet change was also the result of national improvements. From the 1870s all urban social classes enjoyed rising living standards, helped especially by cheaper foodstuffs.

62 *A large house in Molyneux Park Road built after 1891.*

63 *Houses built in the 1890s in Earls Road.*

64 *A large house on the Boyne Park Estate designed by H.M. Caley and developed by the Southborough builder C.J. Gallard after 1893; the façade is highly decorated.*

65 *Houses on the steep Madeira Park on the Eridge Estate begun in the mid-1890s by Beale and Sons; Louis Beale was an architect, developer and builder.*

Late Victorian inventiveness brought the widespread adoption of electric lighting and the telephone, the mass appreciation of cycling and the early use of the motor car. Sports were more widely played and watched. While building activity was respectable in the 1880s, it flourished in the 1890s and 1900s before dropping sharply from 1911. The grant of the title of 'Royal' to the town in 1909 almost coincided with the slowdown in growth.

Housing expanded almost all round the town. There were two new estates on the north-west beyond Mount Ephraim, well described by G. and B. Copus. Five years after the death of F.G. Molyneux in 1886 planning applications began to be submitted on the Molyneux Park Estate, where Molyneux Park Road, formerly a farm track, led to the new Earls and Court Roads. By 1901 there were about 60 households, out of which 23 were headed by people of independent means and the rest by prosperous professional men and tradespeople; altogether they had 124 servants. The Boyne Park Estate was developed from 1893 by a Southborough builder, C.J. Gallard, and it was planned by a local architect H.M. Caley; other architects such as C.H. Strange and C.H. Lander designed individual houses, though Caley was responsible for the huge chimney stacks which were fashionable at the time. It was largely finished by 1910.

In the 1890s Adie had many houses erected in Grosvenor Park, and St James Park was developed at the same time with paired villas. To the east W.B. Hughes designed the Liptraps Estate round Sandhurst Road, well served by the new High Brooms Station of 1893, for property developer F. Peak of Peak Frean the biscuit makers. The scheme of 11 roads and 230 plots was far too ambitious and much was not built on until after 1950. To the south of the town the Abergavenny Estate decided to stop the fall of its income from farm rents through leasing land for building in the new Linden, Madeira and Warwick Parks. While farmland returned £1 an acre, building land fetched as much as £12. The most important firm of builders was Beale and Sons, headed by Louis Beale who was also described as an architect and developer. It began by building four houses in Linden Park in 1886, and 10 more later. They were large, with prominent gables, turrets and balconies and some were fronted with timber or tiles. The firm built 33 out of the 39 houses in Madeira Park between 1893 and 1914. Warwick Park began in 1896 when the local surveyor and auctioneer William Roper F.S.I. advertised for tenders for new roads, sewers and brick pavements; the contract was won by Walter Arnold and Sons of Frant at £13,292. The

Beale firm built 6-36 Warwick Park before 1914; the rest of the 78 houses were erected by Strange and Sons with workshops not far away in Crescent Road, Thomas Bates of Montacute Road and many other builders. Occupants of independent means were joined by commuters using the Central Station. Building continued in the Rusthall suburb, sometimes known as Rusthall New Town, and in the smaller Hawkenbury, both being added to the town in 1900 and where houses for artisans predominated. Shops and other business premises became contiguous along the High Street and Chapel Place and there was more building up Mount Sion. By the 1900s Lonsdale Gardens were built off Mount Pleasant Road, using a large, relatively central site which might have been developed three or four decades earlier.[21]

Housing expansion was matched by several attractive public buildings. Ideally situated at the top of Mount Pleasant, the green-domed Opera House of 1901-2 was built by a company formed by a syndicate in 1897. As the performance of popular drama was disliked by some inhabitants the title of Playhouse was avoided. The auditorium had 1,500 seats. Plays being shown in London appeared as matinees and there were original pantomimes. Among the actor-managers was Frank Benson who specialised in Shakespeare. Concerts and choral works were performed, the

66 *The Opera House opened in 1902 primarily as a theatre, with the adjoining shops and offices.*

singers including Dane Nellie Melba, whose beautiful voice was capable of expansion and stayed extraordinarily even. Political meetings also took place with speakers such as Asquith and Birkenhead. Apart from the theatre there were shops and offices in the large building. It was designed by J.P. Briggs and erected by the firm of John Jarvis of Vale and Goods Station Roads for £31,000, with the fittings and decorations costing £5,000 more. Round the corner in Monson Road the handsome Technical Institute designed by C.H. Strange was opened, again in 1902. It cost £12,000 which was paid for from central and county funds for education. A technical school which it took over had been meeting in other places since the 1880s, with classes run by a Dr Abbott, a retired oculist, and other volunteers. C.R. Fletcher Lutwidge, Mayor in 1895-8 and 1901-2, was largely responsible for the new building. It was capable of holding 800 students. The Tunbridge Wells and Counties Club, designed in Georgian style by Cecil Burns, was opened in 1909, its title perhaps confirming that visitors from London still contributed to the livelihood of the town.

Among other public building a new General Post Office was opened at the corner of Vale and Grosvenor Roads in 1896, replacing the building in the Pantiles in response to the need for a larger building in a more central site. In 1903 the General Hospital had new buildings and the Homeopathic Hospital moved to Church

67 *The new General Post Office of 1895, when it was moved from the Pantiles.*

Road; both continued to rely on voluntary support. A Tunbridge Wells Isolation Hospital was erected in Benhall Mill Road two miles from the town in 1894. As swimming was becoming popular, indoor baths were built in Monson Road in 1898. With rising living standards medical treatment was improving, and the prosperity of the town made local support larger than usual. As train travel grew, a large Central Station building with a clock tower on the Mount Pleasant side was erected in 1912 by the now amalgamated South Eastern and Chatham Railway.[22]

Churches continued to be built as the town expanded and church attendance though declining was still strong. The new Anglican churches were St Matthew in High Brooms (1902), and St Luke (1910), which was designed by E.E. Cronk to be made of brick and stone in an early 14th-century style; for both churches, ecclesiastical parishes were formed. A Friends Meeting House of brick with stone dressings costing £2,100 was opened in Grosvenor Park in 1894 and a small Congregational Church was built in Forest Road, Hawkenbury at the expense of a Mr Le Lecheur in 1898. St John's Free Church on Mount Ephraim, designed by Caley to be built from brick with Bath stone dressings costing £7,560, was erected in 1899 by a building fund created by its minister James Mountain; he had migrated from the nearby Emmanuel Church when he became a convert to adult baptism. Other churches were extended. The Roman Catholic Church had a campanile with a clock added in 1889, and St John's Church

68   *The General Hospital in Grosvenor Road c. 1905-10, after the many alterations of the late 19th-century period.*

was given a new aisle and tower in 1896-7. Frank Chapman has described some of the financial details of this latter work. It cost about £4,000; while subscriptions doubtless provided some of the money, a Royal Bazaar at the Great Hall opened by Mary Duchess of Teck (later Queen Mary) raised £1,200 and there was a big sale at the church.[23]

Equal in importance to the new public buildings was the rapid growth in other physical amenities. The Nevill Ground of 12 acres rented from the Marquess of Abergavenny at £7 an acre was opened in 1898 by the Tunbridge Wells Cricket, Football and Athletic Club; with capital of £10,000 it needed £13,494 to develop the site, thus leaving continued financial problems. The Kent County Cricket Club has played matches there each year since 1901. Since golf, like bowling and tennis, was a middle-class sport, it became popular early on. The Tunbridge Wells Golf Club began in 1890 with nine holes, and the Culverden Golf Club and its Ladies Golf Club began in 1896, all with restricted membership; the Nevill Club of 1914 was open to all. There were football clubs, with the Rangers Football Club and the Tunbridge Wells and District Football League. The bowling

69   *St John's Parish Hall built in the 1890s and called Byng Hall after a noted resident.*

70   *St John's Church in 1904 after its rebuilding in 1896.*

clubs included the Tunbridge Wells Bowling Club which had a green on the St John's Recreation Ground. Roller-skating was available on Culverden Down from 1909, provided by a company. Businesses had their cricket and football teams. The town gained more recreation grounds, partly by gifts of the wealthy. Stone-Wigg gave four acres of Grosvenor Recreation Ground to add to the four acres acquired by the commissioners when they bought the Calverley Waterworks. After his death the family gave £1,750 to buy five acres near St John's Road for a recreation ground which opened in 1900. Thus the relatively newly-built areas benefited like the older dwellings near the Common and the Grove. The town centre was helped enormously by the widening of the bridge at the foot of Mount Pleasant, a combined railway and town work, in 1907.

Out of the sources of power and light, gas stayed at first entirely with the town company, which progressively made streetlighting more sophisticated, introducing Wenham Patent Gas Lamps in the 1880s and new incandescent lamps in the early 1900s; gas became cheaper and spread to almost every household. By 1909 the Crowborough company also served the district, its offices being in the town. The Council was responsible for introducing electricity in 1895. It built a power station in Stanley Road by Grosvenor Bridge in the north of the town, supplying the older, central districts first. As early as 1890, and again in 1904,

71 *The Grosvenor Recreation Ground in 1911; the first after the Grove of 1703, it came partly from the Board's purchase of the Calverley Waterworks in 1865 and partly from Stone-Wigg's bequest in 1899.*

72 *Mount Pleasant in 1905 showing the east side of the station and clock tower before rebuilding in its present form; on the right is an inn, Weekes the drapers, the Great Hall partly concealed, and the shops and houses developed by Adie.*

a company tried to serve the town but was unsuccessful. Water remained a Council responsibility. Supply from the large Pembury reservoir soon proved inadequate; yet since the Groombridge area, drawing on Ashdown Forest, was considered too expensive in 1893, the Pembury seven-acre reservoir stayed the source of supply with six artesian wells being sunk in the next 20 years.[24]

In 1909 *Kelly's Directory* names about 230 or 240 streets, a few having only three or four houses. The number of houses rose from 6,589 in 1901 to 7,507 in 1911, an increase of 13.5 per cent. As has

been seen, since the 1870s most of the business district as distinct from the purely residential areas lay north of the Central Station. By the 1900s the busiest commercial street was the relatively long Camden Road. Next came Calverley and Mount Pleasant Roads. Shops and other businesses continued northwards up Grosvenor and the St John's Roads; they also lay in Goods Station Road off Calverley Road, and on London and Church Roads. South of the Central Station, the High Street and its small adjoining streets and the Pantiles were lined with businesses. Types of businesses and

73 *Calverley Road, a main shopping street in 1907 showing market stalls near where the Market Hall (later the Town Hall) had been.*

professions varied partly according to the street. Besides having the Great Hall and the Opera House, Mount Pleasant Road had the two most important drapers' shops: Weekes lay at the southern corner with Grove Hill Road and Waymarks on the north corner adjoining Calverley Road. Half way along at the top of the hill was Lloyds Bank, formerly Beechings Bank; the Capital and Counties Bank, *Clarendon Hotel* and one of the two Cadena Cafés were also on Mount Pleasant Road. Among the professions in the road were solicitors, physicians, dentists, architects including Caley, auctioneers and accountants, the chief sanitary inspector and the Inland Revenue Office. They outnumbered the high-grade shops, which included chemists, music, china and glass warehouses, a draper, a hosier, a costumier, a bookseller, a photographer, a boot and shoe maker, a provision merchant, dyers and cleaners, fruiterers and grocers. The presence of W.H. Smith and Son at the station is a reminder of the entry into the 20th century. The shorter Church Road with the *Norfolk Hotel* was also almost dominated by the professions, including solicitors and doctors. Shops and other businesses with only a few of the professions, but most of the specialised and luxury shops, lined the Pantiles, the High Street, Calverley and Grosvenor Roads; there were fewer in many other roads such as Mount Ephraim and Grove Hill Road. From the numerous types of trade existing in Camden Road, one would assume a mixed clientele. Working-class customers are suggested

74 *The weatherboarded Pantiles (sometimes known then as 'Ye Pantiles') from the far end in 1905; the former Royal Victoria Hotel and other substantial buildings of the Abergavenny Estate are on the right.*

75 *Opposite: celebrating the 60 years of Queen Victoria's reign on the Pantiles in 1897; there are almost innumerable flags above the butcher's and wine merchant's shops, and a banner 'Gentlemen the Queen God Bless her'.*

76 *The tree-lined Mount Pleasant in 1905; on the left is the sign 'house agent' and 'Stokes [?Dilnott auctioneer] surveyor estate agent valuer': Stokes Dilnott had campaigned for local government reform in the 1880s.*

by the the seven beer retailers out of a total of 119 tradesmen and craftsmen; the 12 butchers, eight grocers, six furniture dealers and seven drapers were probably small businesses which may also have had mainly similar customers. On the other hand the professions were represented by two physicians and surgeons; there was a pianoforte, organ and music warehouse, antique and general furniture dealers, three stationers, a picture framer, photographer and two dining rooms which presumably had a largely middle-class clientele. The two dairies imply the relatively new importance of milk as a drink for nearly everybody, and there were four confectioners and four tobacconists, probably offering products which the working classes were now able to afford. Since this was a main street there were only four men working in building, two plumbers, a joiner and decorator. Altogether the Camden Road had 50 different trades and crafts.[25]

The 49 trades and crafts representing 34 different types in Goods Station Road were dominated by firms linked to the railway. There were three carriers, including a branch of Pickfords, who transported goods between the Wells and neighbouring parishes and the Goods Station; Goods Station Yard had yards occupied by seven coal, coke and corn merchants. While hotels were well distributed in the town, they were found especially along the London Road and Mount Ephraim, taking advantage of views of the Common. The majority of builders were in newer parts of the town; John Marshall had an office in Grosvenor Road and a workshop further to the north in Quarry Road. Workshops needed space and to be near the building sites.

The Rusthall suburb had 49 tradesmen, craftsmen, professional men and managers of rooms. There were two large shopkeepers, a grocer and a draper in the High Street; the other retailers and craftsmen were among the more common types. The four laundrymen and laundresses were probably taking in washing from the rest of the town. For all the main professions Rusthall inhabitants had to use the other establishments in the Wells.

The coming of the telephone proved eventful. In the 1890s the original South of England Telephone Company was absorbed by the National Telephone Company; it was inefficient, with high charges and few subscribers. It was discussed by members of the Tradesmen's Association, especially two chemists, R.A. Robinson of Mount Ephraim and Alfred Nicholson of the Pantiles, who, by the time the Council had secured a licence from the Post Office, had become councillors. Nicholson was chairman of the Telephone Committee which laid down a system for the district. In 1901 the first English Corporation Telephone Exchange was set up, and the town had more telephones and lower charges than any other town, and was linking the surrounding villages. In 1901 the municipal telephone scheme had 500 subscribers and the National Company six hundred. Next year the Council decided to borrow £15,000 to extend its project, which was strongly opposed by a Ratepayers League at the Local Government Board Inquiry. When the National Company bid for the municipal exchange, its offer was accepted. It ran the telephone system until its purchase by the government to include it as part of the post office system in 1912.[26]

77 *A view of most of the houses in Calverley Parade in 1908, with the Opera House now on the other side of Monson Road.*

There were one or two interesting new features among the trades of the town according to the 1909 *Directory*. Shops and other businesses owned by companies with similar outlets across the south-east, in London or much of the whole country were now common. Some of the shops still have familiar names while others have disappeared. Freeman, Hardy and Willis sold 'boots' in two main streets, Mount Pleasant and Calverley Roads; less well-known now was the International Boot Repairing Company on Mount Sion. Grocers were represented by Lipton, the United Kingdom Tea Company, the World's Tea Company and the International Tea Company's stores, the reference to tea implying that it was now the universal drink. Southern Counties Dairies and Maypole Dairy Company suggest the importance of dairy products. Frederick Bateman and Company were opticians. A base in the capital is clear for the London Central Meat Company

The bottom of the High Street in 1906, with a bootmaker, builder [?], and bank on the left and 'art studio' on the right.

and the London Teeth Company. Kentish firms included Fremlin Brothers of Monson Road, based in Maidstone, and the Medway Coal Company with a High Street office and wharf in Quarry Road. Both William Brackett and Sons, who were auctioneers, house and estate agents, valuers and chartered surveyors, and the chartered accountants Creasey, Son and Wickenden, had offices in London. The local banks had been merged into national firms, represented by Lloyds, Capital and Counties and Barclay and Co. The Pearl Life Assurance Company and the Prudential Assurance Company also had offices. Yet most shop businesses had just one outlet with perhaps one, or at the most two, other outlets in Tonbridge, Southborough or Crowborough.

The bicycle and motor car brought new work to the town. Cycles were mass-produced in the West Midlands from the 1890s, and were very cheap. Consequently they were available to almost all classes of society. There were five cycle agents, a cycle dealer who may have held small stocks of various makes as well as obtaining them to order, a cycle repairer, and five cycle makers who probably assembled imported parts; the various names suggest the importance of the trade. In 1896 Messrs George Smith was among English firms laying plant and machinery for cars in their carriage works; yet they were still mainly coach and cart makers. In the 1900s motor cars were beginning to be owned by those members of the upper and middle classes who could afford them, their price still being high. There were two motor garages and five firms described as motor engineers, including G. Stevenson (Kent and Sussex Garage), automobile engineers in the London Road, Autocar Services beginning in 1909 which ran the first regular through bus service to Tonbridge and Hadlow from 1912, and a motor and cycle repairer. However, horse-drawn coaches and

carriages were still much used; there were three coach and carriage building firms, and two carriage works. The latter included Rock, Thorpe and Chatfield which also made cars and had a London connection. The enduring importance of the horse for transport is emphasised by the three jobmasters with livery stables and no less than 16 fly proprietors, a fly being a light, one-horse carriage.

In addition to carriage works, several other manufactures involving perhaps a dozen or a score of workers in each firm may be mentioned. Tunbridge-Ware making continued in a smaller way, with just one manufacturer, Boyce, Brown and Kemp in Camden Road; a depot run by Mrs Porter, presumably selling wares, lay on the Pantiles whilst Barton's on Mount Ephraim was no longer manufacturing and about to close down. The long-lasting firm of Romary made biscuits in Church Road, and there were two scale makers, such as Fairburn Bros. in Camden Road. Finally there

79 *The Frant Road in 1916; the trees may be a little deceptive as on the right, almost hidden, are the houses.*

80 The Commercial Hotel *on the Pantiles in 1913 beside the* Royal Sussex Hotel *which closed in 1880, presumably because of the building of the* Wellington Hotel *and improvement of the* Royal Kentish Hotel.

81 *Vale Road and London Road facing the Common before 1914; the houses were often used for lodgings (by then 'apartments') and small hotels; the tower of Holy Trinity is in the background.*

were at least four firms producing mineral water, including one with the lengthy name of Family Direct Supply Aerated Water Company; presumably there was a large demand from the visitors and more well-to-do residents. Altogether industrial employment was small; lodging the visitors was much more important. There were 34 hotels of varying sizes owned by individuals or companies. According to Savidge the *Earl's Court Family Hotel* on Mount Ephraim, once the home of Molyneux and recently much enlarged with three big storeys on top and an extra wing, offered 100 bedrooms from 1904. Fifteen or twenty rooms were

more usual. There were 54 sets of apartments, 34 lodging houses and five boarding houses; while some were occupied by unmarried residents they were primarily for seasonal visitors. Despite the ubiquitous maids the washing of the prosperous inhabitants, and the visitors, was done by no fewer than 27 laundries, of which 16 were run by women.

As everywhere else in England some of the inhabitants endured overcrowded, insanitary living conditions; the proportion was presumably less than one might expect as there was little industry and so many servants lived in the mansions of the wealthy. Unemployment existed, especially during the winter and in trade depressions. Remedial efforts were led by the one or two Labour councillors and some of the Nonconformist clergy. Plans for a cottage estate by the new Housing Committee around 1900 proved abortive. There was considerable official concern about the workless. From 1891 periodic registers of employers offering work were kept, becoming compulsory in 1905. When a register of the unemployed was begun in November 1907, 130 signed immediately. The mayor had an unemployment fund and individuals were urged to offer work. That these efforts were insufficient is shown by a march on the workhouse at Pembury by about one hundred unemployed in February 1909, which Savidge mentions. The Council began a pensions scheme for its workmen in 1906, three years before pensions became compulsory by the Act of 1909. In 1911 the National Insurance Act introduced contributory unemployment relief, making help compulsory.

82 *Cumberland Villa on Cumberland Walk in 1906; it is one of a pair built about 1830, with rusticated walling, hood-moulds and Gothic glazing bars in the windows, and a porch with clustered shafts. Cumberland Walk was and still remains a quiet backwater in the town centre.*

Education continued to grow at all levels. There were more elementary schools, with 19 Church of England, one Roman Catholic and three non-denominational by 1913. While the Skinners School provided a grammar-school education for boys, the Middle Grade Girls School was taken over by the Kent County Council (KCC), becoming the County School for Girls and in effect a girls grammar school, finally moving from London Road to new buildings at Southfield (1910-13) near St John's Road. The independent Tunbridge Wells High School was run by the Girls Public Day Schools Trust. For adults the KCC appointed H.W. Cook B.Sc as principal to the Technical Institute from 1903; he was also the organising secretary to the KCC Higher Education Committee for Tunbridge Wells and Southborough. Music was extensively taught: there were two schools of music, the Berlitz School and the Tunbridge Wells School of Music, and 12 music teachers. There were three language teachers, artists and a cookery teacher who probably spent part of their time taking classes at the Institute, like some of the music teachers.

In the 1900s a new form of entertainment was offered by a cinema showing silent films. The first dedicated cinema was at the Camden Hall between 1909 and 1924. From 1912 to 1922 the Picture Playhouse at 97 Camden Road showed films, there was a short-lived cinema at the skating rink on Culverden Down in 1913-14, and the Kosmos Cinema in Calverley Road began in 1913. While the cinema was popular almost from the start, it is unlikely to have attracted the huge audiences that it did later.[27]

Clubs, societies and associations together had a broad cultural role. One of the professors of music, Francis J. Foote, who had a studio in Mount Pleasant Road, began a successful choral society in 1903. There was also a choral society and a group of instrumentalists giving concerts led by F.C.W. Hunnibel, organist at St James Church. Thus the teaching of music inspired widespread amateur participation. Public subscription paid for a new bandstand on the Pantiles in 1900 upon which several foreign bands played over the following years. The Tunbridge Wells Literary Society and the Natural History Society continued to flourish and by 1909 there was also an active chess club. Interest in photography reached a peak by the 1900s with the Amateur Photographic Association holding annual exhibitions. There were 13 photographic businesses and several suppliers of photographic materials by 1909. The Tunbridge Wells and South Eastern Counties Agricultural Society continued to hold an annual show; the Farmers Club also remained; gardening did not only focus on the Horticultural Show but also on the popular chrysamthemum gardeners association meeting at the Friendly Societies Hall. Whilst the subscription libraries and the more recent presence of newsagents points to the spread of general reading, there was still no free library by 1914; the Corporation took the preliminary step by adopting the Public Libraries Act in 1895 but without result. While friendly societies and freemasonry continued to grow, trade unions were now well established; the different building trades had their societies, as did shop assistants and postmen; naturally higher wages were a main aim. They were linked by a Labour and Trades Council. Feminist activities may be said to date from 1895, when Amelia Scott formed a branch of the National Union of Women Workers; from 1909 the National Union of Women

Suffragette Societies were holding public meetings, and (being Tunbridge Wells) 'at homes' in the available large houses; in 1913 it had 165 members and many more 'friends'.[28]

Among the unusual events was the holding of the first motor car show in the country in 1895. It was inspired by Sir D.L. Salomons of Broomhill, Mayor in 1894-5. The Agricultural Showground attracted a huge crowd, with many from London, to see his Peugeot and a range of other cars. In 1912-13 the militant wing of the suffragettes, drawn as elsewhere from the prosperous classes, was active following a visit from Sylvia Pankhurst. Two women caused a temporary stir by interfering with a performance on the opera house stage with posters and shouts of Votes for Women. More serious were the throwing of matches into postboxes and the burning of the pavilion on Nevill Ground, which led to an indignation meeting. Both the motor show and the suffragette outbreak were encouraged by the town's national reputation and its relative nearness to the capital.[29]

Among the notable people at this time Stone-Wigg, the first Mayor as well as the last chairman, has already been mentioned; among his outstanding gifts had been the reredos in St Paul's Church, Rusthall, where he was churchwarden; he lived first at Nevill Park and later in Hungershall Park. Sir David Salomons had been called to the Bar, was a High Sheriff and J.P. in Kent, and held various important posts in London companies. As well as having a fascination for cars, he was intrigued by the new electric machines and apparatus, experimenting with them at Broomhill. Solicitors played a significant role in town life. William C. Cripps belonged to a family long established in the town; the eldest son of W.C. Cripps, solicitor and Registrar of the County Court, he became the principal partner in W.C. Cripps and Son of Calverley Road. He was Charter Town Clerk for 36 years, being at the start largely responsible for the long and detailed Improvement Act. He was also Clerk to three other bodies, including the Urban Sanitary Authority. Frank William Stone (1841-1921) was one of the family of solicitors based in Church Road, named Stone, Simpson and Mason from 1900. He was Alderman, Mayor from

83 *The notable mayor of 1894-5, Sir David Salomons of Broomhill, Southborough, who held the first motor car show in the country on the agricultural showground.*

1898 to 1900, for a time Registrar of the County Court (in which office he was followed by his son Neville), and Superintendent Registrar for Births, Deaths and Marriages. His leisure pursuits included membership of the Eridge Hunt. T.F. Simpson had been a partner since 1854 and was the first Magistrates' Clerk of the Commission of the Peace. He had a fine presence and was very influential; he was president of the debating society which met weekly in the Pump Room. He was succeeded as Clerk to the Justices by his son A.T. Simpson, also in the Church Road firm of solicitors. Among several prominent architects were H.H. Cronk and members of his family, and Herbert M. Caley, Mayor in 1908-9, an Alderman and chairman of the Waterworks Committee. Successful businessmen included John Brown of Berkeley Road, Mount Sion, who created Brown's Dairies between the 1870s and 1898, and in the 1900s founded the Nevill Bakery, bakers and confectioners, with shops in Nevill Street and High Street; according to Farthing he was a co-director of the Opera Company and town councillor between 1905 and 1918. Finally there was William Henry Delves (1829-1922), the last prominent member of his family, who was chairman of several local companies including the Gas Company from 1887 to 1920 and clearly a successful manager of businesses; he was Mayor in 1900-1, and a vigilant chairman of the Finance Committee between 1882 and 1922. His hobby was target shooting, being a member of the Tunbridge Wells Rifle Volunteers from its start in 1859. Although the First World War brought enormous changes, the same men provided continuity in the life of the town.[30]

Progress with Vicissitudes

The immediate effects of the First World War were to be seen all over the town. The military presence was almost overwhelming with the assembly of soldiers from all over the country in battalions from 14 regiments before their dispatch to France, and a large camp in Ashdown Forest with the men coming to the town for entertainment. Billets were found for thousands of troops who in effect replaced the lost visitors. According to Strange 'imitation enemies were strung on lines on the Common and in Calverley Park for the recruits to stab with their bayonets' and the churches opened canteens. The hospitals were used for wounded men and V.A.D. centres were opened. The town looked after about 150 Belgian refugees until 1919. While the streets were darkened and evening services dropped, the only damage was that done by a

Zeppelin dropping bombs in Calverley Park which broke many windows.

Sports and cultural activities were curtailed. Building virtually ended. All businesses, the professions and manual work such as domestic employment, gardening and street labour were affected by the enlistment of young men in the Forces. Women replaced them in offices and shops. Women also worked on the land and became nurses; those involved previously in feminist activities led the way in offering their services in war work. The branch of the National Union of Women Workers became the local National Council of Women with Amelia Scott as Honorary Secretary. It supplied street patrols, 18 canteens mainly in houses, a laundry for soldiers and a mending room run by a paid staff and many hundreds of volunteers; they washed for 167,863 men, that is up to 2,500 a week. The first young men in the Forces were the already largely trained Territorials and Yeomanry; they were followed by innumerable volunteers and then in 1916 enlistment became compulsory. A huge number, 776, were killed. From 1919 all churches and institutions had memorial tablets and a War Memorial was erected on Mount Pleasant in 1923. Middle-aged men became special constables and there was a Civil Guard. The end of the War in November 1918 brought a rapid return to peacetime life and conditions; the surviving demobilised men resumed their jobs and business and social activities got underway again.[31]

84 *The War Memorial on Mount Pleasant, 1923; in the house behind were the offices of Siggers and Co. 'Removals and Storage' and Guardian Assurance.*

Despite the lack of population growth in the 1920s and 1930s, and the Depression from 1931, the years were eventful. Turning first to building, more housing was the result of rising living standards, smaller families and fewer servants, and perhaps a preference for new over Victorian dwellings. In 1911 there were 7,507 houses and in 1931 8,391, a rise of 12 per cent, nearly all in the 1920s. One long-term effect of the War was working-class housebuilding subsidised by the ratepayers and national taxpayers at rents manual employees could afford. The Corporation began with 30 houses at Hawkenbury, but was hit by the high price of materials. It planned another estate at Rusthall, where it began building in 1926. By 1939 713 dwellings were erected in various places. Because rents were controlled at a time when most houses were still rented and materials and labour were short, private building began slowly despite the availability of government subsidies. It was modest in the mid- and later 1920s and large in the 1930s, helped by the growth of building societies able to offer mortgages at low rates of interest to the increasing number of owner-occupiers. Some big Victorian houses were converted into flats or demolished to make room for several smaller dwellings; Nevill Court in 50 acres of parkland in Nevill Park was taken down and houses gradually built there. The built-up area expanded in almost every direction. For example,

in the north-east Charity Farm land was developed as the Ferndale Park Estate with Ravenswood and Fairfield Avenues and Hilbert, Lipscombe and Pinewood Roads; the new houses in 1935-6 cost £848 detached and £705 semi-detached. Again in 1927 Culverden House was demolished and its 74 acres auctioned in lots. Sixty-three acres were bought for £25,858 by a company called Culverden Chase, formed by John Egginton and Charles Hillman of the Baltic Sawmills, another instance of money made elsewhere in manufacturing being invested in building; on the land houses were being built in Culverden Park (a road) and Royal Chase by the early 1930s; by 1934 there were 33 householders in Culverden Park and 11, of whom four were doctors, in Royal Chase which held the Culverden Estate Office. By 1934 there were about 260 streets and by 1940 278, showing that building continued strongly until the War.[32]

Two outstanding public buildings were erected in the 1930s. The Kent and Sussex Hospital, which opened in 1934, lay on 11 acres on Mount Ephraim, bought for the purpose in 1927 after the demolition of Great Culverden mansion of 1828. Its

85 *Mount Pleasant in the later 1920s, showing buses when Redcar and Autocar were rival companies, a Redcar advertisement, the front of the Congregational Church, Ruffell and Co. jewellers, the side of the Opera House block and the front of Calverley Parade.*

buildings included not only all the wards and surgeries formerly in Grosvenor Road but also those of the Eye and Ear Hospital on Mount Sion. The local firm of Jarvis built it for £150,000, over 150 workmen being used weekly for two years. It was designed in a modern style by Cecil Burns, with curved exterior ramps to the main wings and using newly developed materials. It followed piecemeal additions and improvements to the Grosvenor Road buildings, including a fully equipped electrical department in 1917, apparatus for treating children suffering from deformities in 1924 and a reconstructed block in 1930. By 1934 there were 23 doctors and eight dentists attached to it. The Homeopathic Hospital which had moved from Upper Grosvenor Road to a large house in Church Road in 1903 stayed in Church Road; a new wing was

built in 1921 and the house replaced by a new building in 1931. It was served by seven doctors and a dentist. Both hospitals had a few private wards. The smaller Eye and Ear Hospital on Mount Sion had four doctors and a dentist attached to it. The Provident Dispensary founded in 1877 continued in Upper Grosvenor Road. They were all in the charge of the Tunbridge Wells, Tonbridge and Southborough Joint Hospital Board of 15 members formed in 1902. While water was drunk on the Pantiles, in 1933 a doctor started the Sherwood Park Clinic based on spring water believed to have special healing qualities.[33]

Although Jarvis claimed that the hospital involved the largest local building contract to date, it was soon at least matched in size by the cost of the unusually comprehensive Civic Centre. On Mount Pleasant and in Crescent Road nearly all of the Calverley Parade and Terrace and their mews which the Corporation had bought in 1895, and some of which it had used for offices, were demolished for the construction of a new Civic Centre. It was designed in 1934 as one great block with a plain brick façade throughout by Percy Thomas and Ernest Prestwich after a nationwide competition. In November 1934 building was precisely estimated to cost £155,550 18s. 5d. with each building priced in terms of cubic feet. The biggest item were the municipal buildings at £65,154 17s. 3d., comprising 744,627 cubic feet at 1s. 9d. per cubic foot. Although work was delayed by the Depression, the Police Court and Assembly Hall in Crescent Road were used from 1939 and the Town Hall on Mount Pleasant, with more space and facilities than in the Calverley Road building, in 1941. For entertainment the Ritz was the only cinema built for its purpose, in 1934, the other cinemas being converted houses. Church building naturally declined with the fall in attendances; there was no new Anglican church and only one new Nonconformist church, a Baptist building in Upper Grosvenor Road in 1938 designed by a local firm, Strange and Grant. A Christian Science Church was built in St John's Road in 1931, described by Savidge as 'a highly original design by Cecil Burns'. St John's Free Church (Baptist) became St Andrew's Presbyterian Church in 1939. Elementary schools were erected in connection with Holy Trinity, St Barnabas's, St Luke's and St Paul's parishes, and in Strange's words 'the Corporation took over the work for defective children carried on by Miss Robbins and other ladies, and built the fine open-air school at Rusthall designed by the late Stanley Philpot'.[34]

The 1920s and 1930s saw the creation of still more parkland which was carefully laid out. Having bought the Calverley Park of

86 *Opposite: the water dippers and people drinking the waters at the well on the Pantiles, 1925.*

87 *The Civic Centre, Crescent Road, Mount Pleasant: the Assembly Hall, Police Station and Courts were opened in 1939, the Town Hall occupied in 1941, and on account of the War the Library, Art Gallery and Museum were delayed until 1952.*

16 acres in 1920, the Corporation provided walks, tennis courts, bowling greens and a bandstand. In 1928 Edward J. Strange of Cadogan Gardens, a J.P., councillor and Mayor in 1936-7, gave four acres in St John's Road for a playing field for schoolchildren opened by the Prince of Wales. Later he gave 23 acres to form part of the Grosvenor Recreation Ground, renamed the Hilbert Recreation Ground in his mother's memory. A donation by H.M. Caley made possible the purchase of a small recreation ground in Rusthall in 1932. Finally in 1936 the Corporation bought about eight acres in Hawkenbury at the other end of the town, providing it with paths, seats and a children's playground. These new parks helped to consolidate the rural, dispersed setting of the town. The creation of parks and open spaces encouraged the growth of a variety of sports. Swimming was not only in the indoor baths in Monson Road, with one tepid bath 90 feet by 35 feet and 10 slipper baths for men and six for women, but also a large open-air bath in the old reservoir. The Nevill Grounds were used for cricket, tennis and croquet. Golf increased on the established courses: in 1934 the Nevill Golf Club had 500 members of both sexes, the Culverden Golf Club had 200 members, Tunbridge Wells Golf Club had 108 members and the Tunbridge Wells Ladies Golf Club 46 members; as fitted the larger membership, the first two had 18-hole courses while the last two had nine-hole courses. As might have been expected there were clubs for all the main sports, such as angling, archery, both types of football, bowls

(as before), squash, racquets, badminton, hockey, cycling, motor cycling and even the flying of light aircraft. There were several packs of foxhounds within reach, the Eridge kennels at Hamsell being especially suitable for Tunbridge Wells hunters. Picturesque scenery on the Common and Rusthall Common and the High Rocks a mile and a half away, and castles such as Tonbridge, Eridge and Penshurst encouraged walking, cycling and more and more motoring.[35]

The annual influx of visitors especially in the summer months had grown markedly since 1909, despite population stagnation. The hotel trade and letting of apartments stayed buoyant. Both the number of sets of apartments to let and that of the hotels and inns had risen over 25 years, to 101 and 49 respectively. Manufacturing employment fell with the disappearance of the making of Tunbridge Ware. In 1916 the business of Boyce, Brown and Kemp of 130 Camden Road was sold to J.T. Ellis who had a shop on the Pantiles called Porter's Warehouse which continued as a retail outlet; the London firm of David H.E. King took over in 1923 to be followed by the Tunbridge Wells Manufacturing Co. in 1924, which collapsed in 1927. One or two workmen produced in a limited way in the town until the 1960s. While the failure to create new designs was one reason for the decline, another was the specialised nature of Tunbridge-Ware production in the face of the growing popularity of the collection of antiques. Mineral water manufacturing was continued by four small firms and A. Romary and Co survived with a shop in Church Road and a factory in Eridge Road.[36]

In 1934 there were at least 11 firms partly or wholly printing, and several firms described as cycle manufacturers or motor-body builders. The number of commuters was growing, with young City men in bowler hats emerging from the Central Station off the 5.50 pm train from Cannon Street becoming a familiar sight by the early 1930s. Otherwise most work came in the professions, trades and crafts serving the townspeople and the inhabitants of nearby East Sussex. Rising living and educational standards among most of the population increased the variety of trades. By 1934 there were 15 newsagents, seven antique dealers (sometimes visited by Queen Mary), three picture dealers and picture frame makers and three shops dealing in the arts, needlework and handicrafts. The popularity of wirelesses brought 17 radio dealers by 1934 and no fewer than 45 motor engineers and garages, and the near disappearance of farriers by the 1930s shows the dominance of motor cars, lorries and vans. There were several chiropodists and more masseuses than in 1909. A shop specialising in baby linen and a 'baby carriage depot' suggests greater care of infants. Finally an agricultural implements dealer, the Farmers Supply Association, and the firm Kentish Farms Ltd are evidence of a market town.[37]

Yet unemployment was severe in the early 1920s when the mayor had an unemployment fund, and through the 1930s as an Unemployed Social Centre with a secretary, reading and recreation rooms and workshops for the unemployed suggest, which only the Second World War brought to an end. This was despite the prospering building industry in the 1920s and especially in the 1930s. Employment in local government and in branches of the Civil Service with local representatives was growing. According to C.H. Strange in 1945 'when the Corporation levied its General District Rate for the first time it was for 1s. 3d. in the pound the total rates being 4s. 5d. They are now 13s. 6d. in the pound'; they were 8s. 6d. in 1934. By 1934 the Corporation paid library and museum staff, and the growing use of water and electricity increased its clerks and technicians; there was an Infant Welfare Centre and the Ministry of Health had a district inspector; an assistant medical officer of health had to be appointed in 1934 because of growing work. Before 1939 there were 65 borough police. The employment of maids, often from neighbouring villages, and dailies by the middle class was still normal as wages were only a little higher than before 1914. Washing was put out to 14 laundries, the majority run by women.[38]

Cultural activities were sustained and expanded. The most important new institution supplying intellectual entertainment was the Public Library which opened in 1921. The town adopted a free library service very late; elsewhere it had often been a 19th-century innovation. The Friendly Society Hall presumably had a book collection available to members of the numerous societies who used it for meetings, and the Mechanics Institute (renamed the Dudley Institute), declining after the creation of the Hall, had a modest library and reading room for which there was a small subscription. Finally its trustees handed it to the Corporation to form a free library; by 1934 it had a reference library, lending library, children's library, newspaper and reading rooms, all still in Dudley Road. Hardly less important was a town museum. Under the leadership of Dr George Abbott a shop was rented in Crescent Road for an educational museum in 1918. It was adopted by the Corporation and moved first to a larger house in Upper Grosvenor Road and then to one on Mount Ephraim. Its curator Dr J.C.M. Given built up general collections particularly representing local geology and botany. There was a wide variety of British and foreign birds, and numerous archaeological and ethnological exhibits.[39]

The Literary Society, the Natural History and Philosophical Society and the Photographic Association flourished, naturally continuing to draw some of their support from the neighbouring villages and countryside. Music was similarly enjoyed by people from East Sussex. While there was no sizeable choral society, there was an annual music festival from 1912 begun by a Mrs Wace. Contributors to its concerts and competitors numbered 250 or three hundred. Mrs Oswald Smith founded a music club in 1929, which often had outstanding vocalists and instrumentalists. The Corporation supported bands on the Pantiles and in the Calverley Grounds, a symbol of the continued importance of leisured inhabitants and the summer visitors; in the 1930s a long list of the bands playing between Easter and September was published. The new art club was supported by the men and women drawing and painting on the Common in the summer. While the growing use of wirelesses kept families at home, cinemas drew them outside in vastly growing numbers. The Kosmos, known familiarly as the 'Kozzy', flourished. When the Ritz at the corner of Mount Pleasant and Church Road opened in 1934 it was called 'Kent's most luxurious theatre' on account of its lavish fittings. With its 15 shops it took 250 workers 20 weeks to build. According to Frank Chapman 'in its original 1,600-seater design, a magnificent three-manual Compton organ rose between films in a glory of sound and light'. Labour and clothing were cheap, so that the cinema was 'served by four projectionists, four magnificently attired commissionaires, 13 usherettes and salesgirls, a page boy and a car park attendant, seats costing 1s. 9d. and 2s. 3d.'. Religious feeling inherited from the Victorian period was seen in the Women's Protestant Union and in the spread of the Gospel overseas in the Tunbridge Wells Branch of the Church of England Zenana Missionary Society, which worked in India and received collections from all the local churches. Devotion to animals is suggested by the Tunbridge Wells Canine Society with dog shows in the Calverley Grounds and the local Fanciers' Association which awarded trophies at annual meetings. By the 1920s temperance societies and rallies were much less evident as drunkenness seemed less of a problem.[40]

Veterans of the First World War were represented by the British Legion and TocH, as everywhere else, and there was also a Veterans' Association Club. The political clubs included the Constitutional Club, the Liberal and Radical Association, Conservative and Unionist Association and, now that women voted, a Women's Conservative and Unionist Association. The now well-established Scouts and Guides abounded as one might expect. Friendly societies had become enormously popular; they comprised, in 1934, the Ancient Order of Foresters with four male courts and a female court and a juvenile branch, all meeting at the hall, a Female Oddfellows' Society, the Independent Order of Comical Fellows, the Tunbridge Wells Equitable Friendly Society with a voluntary and an approved section, and many others. In 1945 the Equitable Society had over 11,000 members and funds worth £1,500,000. For many years the societies held

88 *View of the southern part of the High Street in the 1930s, showing hairdressser 'Louise', Mercer and Co. House and Estate Agents and Goulden and Curry 'Sole Agents for Royal and Corona Typewriters' on the left, and the 'Sports Shop' of A.N. Edwards on the right.*

an annual amalgamation, described as a 'day of country sports and merrymaking'. The Rotary for business and professional men began in 1921 with William Wearing as Founder-President, and there were more masons' lodges; in the 1930s instead of meeting at the Hall, the chapter and five lodges of freemasons met in the Pump Room on the Pantiles.[41]

Local charitable work continued to flourish. In the 1930s the Unemployment Centre and its workshop were supported by voluntary contributions; in 1934 a new year tea party was given for about 120 wives of the workless. At the same time a toy service at St Peter's Sunday school involved local children giving toys and books for the children of St Paul's Stratford, a 'poor parish' in London. The Mayor and Mayoress, R.H. Burslem and his wife,

paid for nearly 3,000 elementary schoolchildren to see films at the Opera House and Great Hall.[42]

From the 1890s 'progressives' led by the Tradesmen's Association had been urging projects enhancing the prestige and prosperity of the town, while from 1901 the Ratepayers League was opposed to more municipal activities in order to keep the rates as low as possible. The former favoured the buying of Calverley Park in 1920, and the latter opposed it. They clashed again in 1922 over a proposed large concert pavilion with an integral bandstand; a modest scheme was finally adopted. Both sides had members on the Council. In 1931 those members of the Council wanting a new Civic Centre lost their seats at local elections to members of the Burgesses' Association, and it was not until 1934 that the scheme was accepted, as already mentioned.[43]

Amelia Scott was one of the first two women councillors, in 1919. Among other notable figures in the town was another member of the Stone family of solicitors, Neville R. Stone (born 1873), who was Registrar of the County Court, Clerk to the Justices for Tunbridge Wells and Frant, and Superintendent Registrar for Birth, Marriages and Deaths. Sir Robert Gower, the son of Alderman J.R. Gower, was for many years on the Corporation and a founder of the old Ratepayers Association. Born in 1880, he became a solicitor in 1903 and continued to practise in the town until the 1940s; he became a councillor in 1909, was an Alderman from 1915 to 1934 and Mayor between 1917 and 1919; among other duties he was a J.P. from 1919, MP from 1924 and chairman of the National Canine Defence League from 1920. The younger C.T. Dodd taught art at Tonbridge School between 1914 and 1927; according to Savidge he exhibited frequently and helped to form the Royal Tunbridge Wells Art Club in the 1930s. Prominent shopkeepers included Councillor W.C. Raiswell of Torrington Villa, Vale Road, who sold groceries, chocolate and confectionery and wines on Mount Pleasant; it developed from 'quite a small shop' to a department store by 1934. A. Norman Edwards had a sports shop in the High Street from the 1930s; born in Hastings, he had worked in a tailor's shop in Cambridge before coming to the town; a handsome man, he was an athlete when young and now coached tennis and golf; for a while he also had a sports shop in Tonbridge. Living in Tonbridge next to his married daughter, his business and coaching in the Wells lasted until the 1960s. Richard Cobb described the shop in the 1930s as 'prestigious', and Edwards standing behind his counter in a blazer as a 'social phenomenon'. Cobb mentioned the 'various dynasties'

of doctors in the 1920s and 1930s, obviously important in a town of numerous well-to-do people: 'On my aunt's recommendation we went first to Old Dr Starling, then to Young Dr Starling; then we switched to Old Dr Ranking, thence to Dr Ranking (his son), thence to Young Dr Ranking (his grandson). The three of them had been in practice for a total of 85 years. Young Dr Ranking, Jack, was a tiny little man – just over five foot – with everything: hands, feet, legs, arms, torso, head, in perfect proportion. He had been cox of the Cambridge boat – the rudder hung prominently in his consulting room – and the fact that he was a "blue" added to the prestige of the practice'.[44]

The new hospital and the Civic Centre in the 1930s were vital additions to the public buildings. The Corporation made up for the inaction of previous decades. The failure to build a major town hall, partly a prestige building, and a large hospital on a suitable site by the end of the 19th century may be due to the lack of local commercial and industrial wealth on the scale of that in parts of the Midlands, Lancashire and Yorkshire. Fortunately labour was still cheap in the 1930s. Once built the work did not have to be repeated, so that public building became a little less important from the 1950s.

89 *The Homeopathic Hospital and Dispensary moved to Church Road in 1903, a wing was added in 1921 and a new building was opened in 1931; there were 27 public beds and three private wards.*

VII War, Recovery and Further Expansion, 1939-1974

The Second World War

The Second World War affected people's lives even more than the First World War. Young men, except those in essential occupations, were conscripted; single women and married women without children joined the Forces or worked in the Women's Land Army or munitions' factories; others replaced men in offices or in transport such as buses and trains. Men in local jobs became special constables, joined the Home Guard to help protect the country against invasion, or the Auxiliary Fire Service and the A.R.P. to deal with bombing, which resulted in their leisure time being curtailed. Food rationing began in January 1940 whilst petrol for private use was first limited to driving 200 miles per month and then stopped from March 1942. The 'blackout' involved street lighting and the covering of shop and house windows. Shelters as protection against bombing were universal.

Only 166 of the Tunbridge Wells men in the Forces were killed. Servicemen were estimated to have smoked 48,000 cigarettes sent by the local War Comforts Association and by 1944 wore over 35,000 garments provided by the Knitting Society.

Despite the policy of appeasement, the country had been preparing for war for two or three years before its outbreak on

3 September 1939. Inhabitants were made aware of the horrors of Nazism by the flight of young Jewish children from Prague in 1938, who were housed in many places across England such as Beacon House in Rusthall. On account of the government's concern about a possible gas attack, respirators were issued locally as elsewhere for adults and children in 1938-9. To deal with bombing there was an appeal for air raid precautions wardens; an A.R.P. HQ was set up at 81 London Road and from May 1939 a network of depots was created. At one time there were 45 full-time and 500 part-time wardens. Part of the cost of the A.R.P. during the War was borne by the Corporation. From September shelters were made in cellars of firms, in houses and gardens and in trenches on the Calverley Grounds and the Common. According to Alastair Noble, in the end there were 70 public shelters to hold about 7,000 people, and 2,700 more could be crammed into school shelters. In the Home Guard, which formed in 1940, the local companies comprised the 22nd Battalion (Tunbridge Wells) Kent Home Guard. Other men not enlisted joined the well-supported Special Constabulary. The Kent and Sussex Hospital was camouflaged, and, whilst acting as an emergency medical services hospital in case of invasion, plans were made to accommodate 668 patients, many to be on mattresses between beds and in the corridors. Though the town was not targeted by German aircraft, stray high explosive bombs and incendiaries killed 15 people and seriously injured 70, destroying 13 houses and badly damaging ninety-eight. The worst months were September, October and November 1940, the worst raid being on 12 September when bombs were dropped in a line from Connaught Way to Great Culverden Park, then from the hospital (destroying the casualty ward) to Grosvenor Road. After over two years without incident, a bomb caused injuries and much house damage in May 1943, and six flying bombs fell in the summer of 1944.

The XII Corps consisting of two divisions of about 20,000 or 25,000 men defending Kent and Sussex had its HQ in the town, the GOC being stationed at 10 Broadwater Down; nos. 2 and 13 were Army billets, Dunorlan House was occupied by the Army as well, and other houses were used as an auxiliary hospital and evacuees hostel. When General Montgomery was GOC in 1941 he sent his staff officers on morning runs. The Mechanised Transport Corps were in Birling Road. The Emmanuel Church on Mount Ephraim had a canteen for the Forces, 600,000 or 700,000 being served in six years. The busy Women's Volunteer Service ran the mobile canteen.

Throughout the War the Civil Defence Commissioner for South East England was stationed in Bredbury mansion on Mount Ephraim. The town was run by the Council helped by an Emergency Committee of four with the Mayor, Alderman C.E. Westbrook of the firm of auctioneers, as chairman. Rationing was controlled by a divisional food office in Mount Ephraim House on Bishops Down.

The absence of young men and women in the Forces and of visitors was partly balanced by the presence of evacuee children from the London area. At the start 5,000 arrived in three days; the majority went home by the end of 1939 as London had not yet been bombed. According to Ann Bates in January 1940 there were 855 children, often moving once or twice, many of whom remained for two or three years. Pupils of the Blackheath High School for Girls were taught at the Tunbridge Wells High School for Girls, the Lewisham Colfe's School for Boys were at Skinners, and the Bluecoat School at Culverden House. Guy's Medical School occupied several houses in the north-east of the town, lectured students were in the new Baptist Tabernacle in Upper Grosvenor Road and also used Pembury Hospital. In the summer of 1944 when flying bombs were a danger, local children were sent to the West Country for several months. In addition to paying higher rates and taxes, townspeople were encouraged to save by war saving drives, such as the 'Spitfire Fund' of 9 August to 29 September 1940 which raised £5,031 and the War Weapons Week of 13-20 December 1940 which made £510,224. Up to December 1944 £8,207,510, the equivalent of £230 a house, was saved. There were salvage drives collecting waste paper and metals including railings. Householders were encouraged to grow their own vegetables in their gardens and to rent allotments, the number of which much increased. Part of the Culverden golf course was ploughed. There was an agricultural show each year at Down Farm off St John's Road, no doubt to help farmers. Leisure time was reduced by people working longer hours, Home Guard and C.D. duties, and sport was severely curtailed. Yet half the population went to the four cinemas, and there were regular shows in the Assembly Hall with its 1,142 seats; on one evening in April 1943 it was praised as having the 'best boxing show in Tunbridge Wells', with an exhibition bout between the welter-weight champion of Great Britain, RAF Sergeant Ernie Roderick, and his usual sparring partner RAF Sergeant Cooper.

Three years before the War ended the Corporation asked the Civic Association to prepare a Post-War Development Scheme, which was ready by 1945. A principal proposal was the revival of the Pantiles as a commercial, social and cultural centre, with a self-supporting repertory theatre, museum and art gallery, winter garden and underground car park. It was abortive. By late 1944 with the expulsion of the Germans from France, there were signs of the relaxation of wartime effort at home. In September house windows could show lights again and in October the Home Guard ended. By early 1945 some of the C.D. groups were closing. The unconditional surrender of Germany in May and of Japan in August were celebrated by church services, street parties, parades, dancing on the Pantiles and official and unofficial bonfires on the Common. On 24 June the mayor took the salute at a 'stand-down' parade of the C.D. services in the Calverley Grounds, thanking them profoundly on behalf of the Council and the Emergency Committee.[45]

Post-War Recovery

Full employment continued after the War as the civil service and local govenment work grew. Professions such as teaching and medicine expanded, and there were more shops as incomes rose. Maids earning low wages in middle-class homes disappeared, though daily helps working shorter hours for higher wages survived. Instead many housewives had hoovers and washing machines. A few wealthy households had resident housekeepers. Most young women were shop assistants, clerks and secretaries. The town continued to attract almost as many visitors as before because of its popularity as a conference centre. Retired people still settled in the town; in 1951 the town had a much higher proportion of elderly than in the whole of Kent, with only Herne Bay and Whitstable having a higher percentage. Because there were almost no servants living in prosperous homes and retired people were mainly middle-class, one would expect this social group to be larger than in most towns.

PERCENTAGE DISTRIBUTION OF THE POPULATION BY AGE[46]

Ages:	under 15	15-64	65 and over
Tunbridge Wells	19.4	62	18.6
Average in Kent	22.5	65.4	12.1

Some years elapsed before there was a full return to peacetime conditions. Rationing of food was more severe than in the War, and did not end until 1954. In 1947 coal was rationed and vegetables were scarce. On the other hand the elderly and infirm benefited from 'meals on wheels' provided by the W.V.S., the town being the first in Kent with this service, perhaps reflecting the large number of cars owned locally. People with higher incomes benefited from restaurant meals, and those of them who travelled to Hastings by rail from buffets reopened in 1946. Petrol for private cars became available again in 1945, only to be stopped for a year in 1947. According to Ann Bates 120,000 people applied at this time to the local Regional Petroleum Office, created in 1939, for coupons. When it closed in 1950, 130 permanent and 120 temporary staff became redundant. The Kent and Sussex Hospital had a shortage of nurses and financial problems which led to the closure of three wards in 1947. In 1949, 386 nurses were needed now that the health system was nationalized.

As there was no building during the War, in 1945 4,000 needed homes. In 1946 the Council were planning estates off Powder Mill Lane at the Southborough end of the town, and off Eridge Road on the south side (known as the Ramslye Estate). The Powder Mill Lane Estate was being built by 1947; in 1950 the Cunningham, Montgomery and Tedder Roads had 115 occupied houses; only housing in Tedder Road was not quite completed. The Ramslye Estate was intended to have 400 houses, with at least eight shops, a school, community centre and public house. The first 62 houses were occupied in 1949; only two contractors had tendered and the Council was considering the use of direct labour. Next year there was still a shortage of building labour and the Ramslye Estate was delayed by the lack of cement. The Council discussed a new estate of 394 houses where Pembury and Sandhurst Roads met. There was little private building in the later 1940s; it was controlled and also restricted by the shortage of labour and materials. As these factors eased in the early 1950s building revived. Builders in 1949 had to compete with the government for bricks, the High Brooms Brick Works contracting in February to supply 3,000,000 hand-made facing bricks for a power station at Southwick near Brighton. By 1950 there were about 286 streets, only eight more than in 1940.

Recovery was quicker in entertainments. All the sports started again in 1946. At Cricket Week Kent suitably beat Sussex by an innings, there was the Open Tennis Tournament in July, football began in the autumn, there was a bowls tournament and finally Bonfire Night. By 1955, 11 different sports were played, half of them by two or more clubs. The Eridge Hunt was thriving. There was also a rambling club serving not only the town but also Southborough and Tonbridge and neighbouring villages. The Motor Club continued, holding a Festival Rally in 1951. As incomes rose for most people, car ownership spread so that traffic had become a problem in the shopping streets by 1950. The purchase by the Corporation of the Dunorlan Estate near Pembury Road provided a new 30-acre pleasure ground with a huge lake for public pleasures, thus increasing the parklands as the town expanded. In 1950 a fête held there attracted 10,000 people.[47]

Cultural activities were represented by many clubs and associations; among them music flourished as earlier, provided by the Orpheus Male Voice Choir and the Choral Society giving concerts, and the Symphony Orchestra with Sunday concerts in winter including distinguished guest artistes; there was an Amateur Operatic and Dramatic Society, a drama club and other amateur dramatic clubs thus suggesting that acting and playgoing was becoming popular; there was also an annual Drama Festival of One-Act Plays in the autumn. Military and brass bands still played on the Pantiles and in the Calverley Grounds in the summer, and there was an annual band contest in May. The Photographic Society, chess and art clubs continued, and there were poetry, philatelic and film societies. Cinema shows at the Opera House, Kosmos and Ritz were still very

90 *A modern view of the Calverley Grounds, planned in 1829 as part of the Calverley Estate; the best reminder of the extensive, park-endowed character of the town.*

popular with television sets still in a minority of homes. The agricultural shows continued until 1950, and from 1951 the Tunbridge Wells and Southern Counties Agricultural Show was revived on the Eridge Road site. The Constitutional Club and the Civic Association remained; the still numerous leisured and professional men in particular filled the Kent and Sussex Club and Tunbridge Wells and Counties Club. Societies with charity as well as conviviality among their aims were well represented by the Inner Wheel, Round Table and Rotary Club. While women were numerous in the music, drama and art societies, they had their own Ladies' Residential and Women's Constitutional clubs. Employers were represented by an active Chamber of Trade and workers by the vocal Trades and Labour Council.

91 *Church Road in 1955, showing the Ritz cinema and Holy Trinity as well as houses on the north side of Church Road; hotels and houses on Mount Ephraim beyond the Common are visible in the distance.*

For most of these activities the Assembly Hall was used. Its theatre also held pantomimes and variety shows. Its ballroom had old-time and modern dancing, sometimes to well-known visiting dance orchestras. The hall was also hired for private functions, such as dances, shows, meetings, bazaars and exhibitions, to some of which the general public was admitted. Outdoor activities on the Pantiles included old-time dancing, plays and art exhibitions, the nearest approach to the proposals of the Post-War Development Scheme.[48]

Among trades, crafts and manufacturers by 1950 A. Romary Co. still made biscuits and three mineral water manufacturers continued, though Tunbridge-Ware making had practically disappeared. There were still two scale and weight makers in Calverley and Camden Road, and at least four other makers such as a scientific instrument maker and umbrella manufacturer, working with tiny staffs.

While manufacturing was almost insignificant, many trades reflected the needs of the large, prosperous middle class and of visitors. There had been a surge in antique dealing with now 16 dealers of whom seven were on the Pantiles, and to whom visitors were especially attracted. Stamp collecting was now popular, as seen not only by the society but also by two philatelist shops; they almost overshadowed the seven photographers. Many shopkeepers were both stationers and booksellers, and there were subscription libraries at W.H. Smith and Boots. The 11 printing firms included the long-established Hepworth and Co. of Vale Road and the Courier Printing and Publishing Co. There were no fewer than 42 cafés, restaurants, tea-rooms and dining rooms which drew people wanting to buy meals while food was rationed, as well as those visiting the town for a few days.

Clothing still involved great expenditure. Weekes and Waymarks remained the leading department stores, with Waymarks having a near 20th-century neighbour in Sibthorpes, now W.M. Sibthorpe and Son, a 'fancy drapers, ladies' and children's outfitters'. There were 88 other drapers, outfitters, tailors and other suppliers of clothing. Four wool stores and three baby linen shops accompanied them, and furnishing was again represented by suppliers of various types.

The engineering trades were naturally dominated by wirelesses and motor cars. There were 29 electrical engineers and, among other types, 28 motor engineers and garage owners. There were also three motor-tyre dealers. Fruiterers and wine merchants were notable among food and drink tradesmen. In addition to numerous doctors and surgeons, an osteopath, four physiotherapists and eight chiropodists provided specialised medical treatment, being more in number than before the War.

Altogether retailers and the professions were increasing and becoming more varied. While food was rationed and housing was inadequate, rising salaries and wages and the return of normal leisure time encouraged high consumption after wartime shortages and forced saving by the numerous prosperous middle class and neighbouring country dwellers.

The expansion of local government and the civil service was seen in the increase of public servants in the town. The staff of the Corporation and the number of ministry employees with offices grew; in 1950 the latter included representatives of the ministries of agriculture and fisheries, education, food, health, labour and national service, national insurance, transport and works; some were south-eastern regional officials showing that in one respect the town was a regional capital. Income tax officers existed as before, some of whom dealt with a wide area as well as the temporary War Damage Commission. The Kent County Council also had local representatives. Finally the Civil Defence Regional Centre was situated in Bredbury into the 1950s.

The number of hotels had shrunk to 42 and the number of apartments to let to 18; visitors staying for at least several weeks were fewer since the War. On the other hand the town was popular as a conference centre, especially with the availability of the Assembly Hall adding to the attraction of the scenery and climate. In 1949 2,000 came to a British Legion County Rally. The full equality of women outside the home was seen in the election of Miss Muriel Wells, who had been the local W.V.S. representative in the War, as the first woman Mayor in 1949. Signs that life was returning to normal were the shopping week and the first carnival since 1937 which took place in 1951.[49]

Further Prosperity and Expansion

The standard of living grew for nearly everyone with full employment in the 1950s and '60s. The slow rise in population of the 1930s was resumed in the 1950s; from 35,367 in 1931, it grew to 38,397 in 1951 and 39,861 in 1961. It accelerated during the 1960s to 44,506 in 1971. One reason for the rise was the growth in commuting, particularly by train to London in under an hour; rail fares were still low and housing in a fashionable country town was much cheaper than in suburban London. In 1961 according to Savidge 4,000 persons who lived in the town worked elsewhere, half travelling by train. 'British Rail figures for 1973 show nearly 2,000 holding season tickets to London from the Central Station and 270 to Tonbridge, among other destinations in Kent and Sussex towns.' Most of the men were businessmen, financiers, lawyers, administrators and clerks, and the women mainly young secretaries and clerks who were single or married without children. If one considers their families they represented 8,000 or 10,000 people, perhaps a fifth of the population. The large leisured group remained the other unusual part of the population. In 1971, 9,850 people, or between 22 or 23 per cent, were retired; now the highest proportion of any Kentish town. On the other hand there were only a few visitors for two or three weeks or more who drank the waters, listened to the band in the day and concerts in the evening, and walked or drove in the surrounding countryside; presumably holidays at the British seaside and overseas instead of at inland spas were more attractive for nearly everyone. Visitors for a day, or staying one or two nights, perhaps on the way to the Sussex coast, were still common. Savidge suggests that, out of nearly 20,000 town jobs, about 6,500, or one third, were done by men and women living outside it. The country was slightly cheaper, and more attractive to many families, and trains, buses and particularly cars which more and more people owned made the town easily accessible from villages 10 or 15 miles away, and even the Sussex coast. Of course the town had long been an attractive shopping and entertainment centre.[50]

House building flourished from the early 1950s. It developed much faster than population growth as dwellings in main streets were demolished or converted into shops, mansions with big gardens were replaced by a group of small houses, rows of dwellings were erased for car parks and a few Victorian housing estates were condemned as squalid and cleared. Households were smaller on average as the number of broken marriages grew and more men and women lived singly. Council-house building

92 *Calverley Road, a principal shopping street in the 1950s. On the left side of the street is Timothy Whites and Taylors Ltd, a chemist and ironmonger, F.W. Woolworth and Co, a national store selling an almost endless variety of cheap goods, and Currys the cycle dealers, also with many branches.*

became large, with 2,782 one-, two-, or three-bedroomed homes as small houses and flats, for over 12,000 people by 1974. As the dwellings were new and rents were subsidised, the housing manager was always under pressure; at that time there were 3,200 on the waiting list. By then there were 16 estates, mostly in the north-east near Powder Mill Lane, High Brooms and Sherwood off Sandhurst Road (1,357 homes), Ramslye, and Showfields (the latest) on the former Agricultural Showground in the south-west (764 homes) and the Lower Green area on the north of Rusthall (486 homes) in the west. There were 48 houses on the Windmill Fields site cleared about 1960, and 37 in the St James area, 24 post-war pre-fabricated homes at Hawkenbury, and 56 houses elsewhere. On the Sherwood Estate, which was the largest estate, 14 new roads had been constructed by the early 1960s, or about a quarter of the new roads started round the town.

Private building recovered sharply in the 1950s after controls were lifted and labour and materials became sufficient, continuing at a higher level through the 1960s and early 1970s; it was based on the rising population, especially that of commuters, and the further growth of small households as more marriages were split by divorce. The clearance of older small houses for car parks north of Calverley Road and elsewhere as sites for businesses including garages, and the demolition of 10 houses in Broadwater Down, and others in the Pembury Road for smaller housing were also important. New private building was noticeable, for example between the Sherwood Estate and the Pembury Road, and in the south in the area of Broadwater Down. By 1963 the number of roads was about 342, 57 more than in 1950, and in 1974 about 413, 71 more than in 1963.

There were many new public buildings, such as the glass-covered Land Registry at Hawkenbury, the government Merevale building in London Road, the PPP block of offices and the Telephone Exchange at the Culverden, all rather dull-looking. The Pump Room on the Pantiles was demolished in 1964 for a Union House, as was the Roman Catholic Church for a building on the site of a 19th-century house off Crescent Road in 1974-5. £250,000 was spent in 1967 and 1968 on a multi-storey car park typical of larger towns, which was erected on part of the existing car park by Monson Road. Sandown Court, the home of Sir Robert Gower until his death in 1953, became a secondary school. However, some older public buildings, including churches, were demolished for shops, offices and car parks. The old Town Hall in Calverley Road made way in 1959 for Sainsburys and the Roman

Church for a supermarket whilst the Emmanuel Chapel of the Countess of Huntingdon was removed for hospital parking. Mount Ephraim House became a W.V.S. Residential Club for retired people of limited means. The listing of buildings of architectural or historical interest under the Town and Country Planning Acts, the views of the Civic Society and amenity societies, and individuals supporting conservation helped stop further destruction of older houses and public buildings.[51]

The economy and society of the town continued to change. The number of visitors in the summer for several weeks or more fell sharply. By 1974 the *Directory* listed only five sets of rooms to let and 24 hotels. Its role as a market town serving north-east Sussex remained without becoming more important. Savidge suggested that about four per cent of the employed inhabitants were linked to farmimg, such as agricultural engineers and consultants, one or two corn merchants and farmers in the suburbs. Although the scale makers and Romarys had gone there were, among other firms, two mineral water processors, and a maker of invalid chairs and surgical appliances. While manufacturing near the town centre was minimal, an industrial estate was emerging in the High Brooms valley to take advantage of larger sites. This had been proposed in the 1945 Development Scheme. In Longfield Road the Milk Marketing Board transport depot and two manufacturing firms appeared in 1958. By 1963 the road contained Robert Stace and Co, printers run by D.P. Chalklin which had been in Mount Sion, scientific instrument makers Bellingham and Stanley, and J. Rawson and Sons, commercial motor-body builders who had also moved from nearer the town centre. Seven other firms were new to the town. In 1974 there were still 10, mostly manufacturing, businesses. Beyond the borough boundary in High Brooms beside North Farm Road there were nine manufacturing, trading and transport firms before the War and between 11 and 13 in the 1950s; the number rose to 15 in 1963 and 31 in 1974. If these firms are considered part of the economy of the town by the 1960s, light industry was at last making a considerable contribution to local employment.

The town continued to develop as an administrative and service centre both in relation to the county, to the south-eastern counties and to the whole country, where relative proximity to London was important. By 1974 among the Kent County Council offices were those of the Kent Education Committee (West Kent Divisional Executive), the Kent Education Committee Youth Employment Bureau, and the KCC Social Services Department and Maintenance Division, all at 39 Grove Hill Road; there was also the Kent Fire Brigade, the County Constabulary, the KCC Old Peoples Home in Sandown Park and the Old Ladies Home in Sandhurst Road; maternity, midwifery and home nursing were also the responsibility of the KCC elsewhere in the town. Those services which were also provided in Southborough and Tonbridge only related to the town and neighbouring rural area; those services absent in these towns served all south-west Kent. The Inland Revenue (District Valuer and Valuation Office), Europa House in Church Road served south-west Kent, whilst the Inspector of Taxes served the neighbouring countryside, and probably Southborough as well as the town. The home counties benefited from the South East England Tourist Board in Monson Road and the Inland Revenue Licensed Property Valuer and the Superintending Valuer (South Eastern Region) in Merevale House, London Road. Post Office Telephones in Telephone House, Church Road had a regional wing training centre in Hawkenbury. Private services included 20 insurance offices concerned with personal property, real estate, accidents and death, and the Private Patients Plan with a managing director, secretary and numerous staff in Eynsham House, St John's Road, which administered private health insurance for people all over the country. Among car and garage businesses in several towns, Caffyns from Eastbourne bought a large garage in St John's Road in 1945.

The large number of certain types of shopkeeper reflects both the unusual proportion of prosperous residents, the dependence on the town of neighbouring villagers, and passing visitors. In 1974 there were no fewer than 29 antique dealers, 11 jewellers and three stamp dealers, the only ones in south-west Kent. The popularity of drawing and painting was served by five art material dealers, and that of dancing by three dancing schools. The keeping of dogs, cats and other pets had been growing since the War; there were six pet and three dog beauty stores. More and more people had been owning motor cars: one would expect the number of motor cars in and round the town to be unusually large; there were 43 garages dealing in and repairing cars. There were 10 nurserymen, garden centres and florists, with 13 fruiterers. Small shopkeepers included 13 confectioners and nine tobacconists. Thirty-six restaurants, including ones serving Chinese meals, cafés and bars suggest that eating outside the home was popular. The furnishing and clothing trades were also prominent. There were 14 fancy goods dealers, which included toys and leather goods. Thirty-three rug and carpet dealers, upholsterers, suppliers of fabrics and other furniture dealers were joined by 24 outfitters, including dealers in sports and riding equipment, 19 fashion specialists, seven wool and eight boutique shopkeepers.[52]

The solicitors served the town and the neighbouring countryside, and perhaps some of the people in Southborough though not many in Tonbridge. To the extent that boys of the town attended Tonbridge School as day boys the town used Tonbridge, there being no comparable public school in the town, despite the presence of St George's (private) School in Pembury Road and Calverley Park Gardens. The Skinners School and the Girls Grammar School and the other secondary schools served the neighbourhood as well as the town. Eleven or twelve new schools, of which four or five were secondary, opened between 1952 and 1974, and there were extensions and improvements to existing schools, overcrowding and unsuitable rooms becoming worse after the War when building was delayed six or seven years; the baby boom of the mid-1940s put further pressure on accommodation in the mid- and later 1950s, and building continued until the early 1970s without a pause as population grew. The first new schools, opened in 1952, were the Bennett Memorial (Church of England) Girls Secondary School and the Huntleys Boys Secondary School, both at Culverden Down. The pre-War Tunbridge Wells Technical School and College of Art became the expanded West Kent College of Education and the separate School of Arts and Crafts, the former finally becoming the West Kent College of Further Education. One or two state schools closed, such as King Charles School in 1970, presumably because of cramped or dated accommodation.[53]

Though the Girls High School closed in 1945, Kent College at Pembury became larger and there were two private girls' schools in the town. The town's major contribution to the professions was the Kent and Sussex Hospital, with a new Postgraduate Wing in 1973 costing £70,000, the gift of the doctors, the public and the Homeopathic Hospital still separate in Church Road, and the doctors and nurses who worked there. Patients came not only from the countryside but also Tonbridge and Southborough, the former's largely low-lying ground making it rather less suitable for curing sickness and disease; its relatively small Cottage Hospital and the Pembury Hospital being on hills. With the many administrators in public and private institutions and the managers of shops and businesses, the town almost overflowed with professional men and women who worked in it, apart from the professional people among the commuters.

Conclusion

The town has developed further since 1974. That the more rapid growth of the 1960s and early 1970s continued is shown by the fact that the population rose to 61,000 in 2001, an addition of almost 40 per cent. As families have continued to grow still smaller with more single mothers and divorced couples, a disproportionate number of houses and flats has had to be built. The number of roads rose from about 413 in 1974 to about 535 in 2005. While housing did not extend much beyond the existing edge of the town, it filled numerous closes and short roads in the suburbs. There have been changes to the public buildings. The Kent and Sussex Hospital expanded by the demolition of Emmanuel Church as a car park site in 1974, a new casualty department costing the relatively small sum by modern standards of £50,000 and the Culverden Wing for £8,200,000 in 1985. Holy Trinity Church has become an Arts Theatre and, sadly, the neo-Norman church was mistakenly replaced by a building thought to be more suitable for modern needs. A second boys' grammar school, reflecting the need for the more academic secondary school education as numbers grew, was founded near the boundary with Southborough. As everywhere else supermarkets were important by the 1970s, taking business from small shopkeeping by confectioners, tobacconists, fishmongers, butchers, grocers and greengrocers. The Royal Victoria Place, a typical shopping arcade with 100 shops including a department store, was opened in 1992, confirming the Calverley Road area as the heart of the trading centre. The Ritz (Essoldo) Cinema was closed and has now been demolished. Yet the High Street and the Pantiles remains the centre of specialised shops such as boutiques and those selling antiques and jewellery. Its restaurants have drawn customers from a wide area, as well as passing visitors. The Place reflects the growing use of motor cars for shopping, concentrating it in major towns to the detriment of smaller centres such as Southborough and Tonbridge. The Pantiles and Common have stayed, perhaps grown further, as major tourist attractions due to the pedestrianised nature of both as well as their distinctive beauty, the drinking of the waters on the Pantiles and the sloping site of the Common from the top at Mount Ephraim. The Nevill Ground has continued to host cricket and sport; it is now almost the only place where first-class Kent cricket matches are played apart from at the home ground at Canterbury, other grounds ceasing to be used in the 1990s. The professions such as teaching, the law, medicine and administration grew as the town expanded, with the exception of the clergy, the Anglican churches failing to replace curates and the Roman Catholic Church its priests, as religious worship further declined.

Finally some general themes about the relatively short history of the town may be mentioned. Three periods seem especially significant. In the 1680s the Pantiles shopping and entertainment centre and the lodging houses of Mount Ephraim and Mount Sion were created. The visitors led by Princess Anne, the aristocracy, gentry and businessmen sought health from drinking the waters and fine air and pleasures in a novel rural environment. The tradesmen and craftsmen serving their needs soon became permanent inhabitants. In the 1830s the Calverley Estate was almost completed and smaller building schemes were successful. While visitors remained important, the rise in population of about 40 per cent confirmed the character of the town as a residential centre for men and women of independent means, including the retired. The new layout of housing in terraces, villas and crescent villas in a park coincided with major advances in the design of Tunbridge Ware. As the wealth of the inhabitants and visitors rose with the growth of numbers, the demand rose for not only attractive living conditions but also beautiful possessions, encouraging the makers to produce higher quality wares. Finally in the 1930s the well-named Kent and Sussex Hospital serving the Wells, the

93 *A modern view of Brighton Lake, dug for children in 1858 at the suggestion of the Revd W.L. Pope to give work to the unemployed, and popularly known as 'Pope's puddles'; a pleasant addition on the edge of the Common.*

neighbouring country and towns and the comprehensive Civic Centre were built. London commuters became an established section of the inhabitants.

Down to the 19th-century London merchants, professional men and financiers speculated often successfully in developing the buildings and amenities. Their capital was joined by that of the inhabitants of Tonbridge town and neighbouring landowners and prosperous farmers. In the late 19th and 20th centuries investment came from businesses elsewhere in Kent and in Sussex as well as London. First the visitors, then the leisured residents with them, and more recently the commuters with the retired people have ensured the existence of the town by spending there incomes made in the capital, elsewhere in England and sometimes overseas.

The service of the visitors largely from London between about 1680 and 1780, created a local population dominated by numerous lodging housekeepers and retailers. From the later 18th century they were joined by a relatively prosperous class of retired professional and business men and single women and widows of independent means. They were able to afford large, often detached houses in spacious gardens and often adjoining the Common or parkland. As church attendance was the fashion among the Victorian middle class, churches and chapels flourished on account of the continuing stream of visitors as well as the leisured residents. Funerals were unusually well supported. As the middle class dominated the literate section of the population local newspapers flourished from the 1850s. Playgoing was important around 1800 and also about 1900 when the Opera House was built. Leisure encouraged club life on the lines of London clubs, which led to three public buildings between 1870 and 1909. There was the Literary Society from 1836, the later subsidised Mechanics Institute, and other cultural societies. People had time to express divergent views on local matters, at meetings and especially in the newspapers. Again, charity was strong from the end of the 17th century to the present day on account of prosperous visitors and residents. A few people used the wealth they had made elsewhere to make huge contributions to local welfare. From the Grove in 1703 the parks were the gift of the rich. The hospital expanded again and again before its final rebuilding, supported by voluntary means. Men out of work in winter or during a depression were extensively supported by soup kitchens or the artifical provision of work by the well-to-do. Finally though the town was the creation of its visitors and later its leisured inhabitants it came to serve the surrounding area like a market town. People in the country used its shops and professions; they enjoyed its entertainments, from the 1830s read its newspapers and joined its cultural societies. In this way the town was like Bath in the 18th century and Cheltenham in the 19th century. Its 20th-century commuters reinforced its prosperous middle-class character, spending locally money earned in London. They made it like Brighton, Margate and Ramsgate and the other large seaside resorts of Sussex and Kent.

Notes

Part One: The Rise of the Spa Town, 1680-1835

1. R.V. Lennard, 'The Watering Places', in Lennard (ed.), *Englishmen at Rest and Play: Some Phases of English Leisure* (Oxford, 1931), p.18.
2. National Archives Map of Wybarne Estate, *c.*1570; P. Hembry, *The English Spa, 1560-1815: A Social History* (1990), pp.44-8, 60-1; Hembry referred to C.W. Chalklin, *Seventeenth Century Kent, A Social and Economic History* (1965), pp.157-8, based on Chalklin, 'A Kentish Wealden Parish, Tonbridge, 1550-1750', Oxford B.Litt thesis (1960), pp.101-5; the source of the comments on the developments of 1636 and 1638 is T.B. Burr, *The History of Tunbridge Wells* (1766), p.53. The date of Henrietta Maria's visit is sometimes stated to have been 1630.
3. Lennard, pp.46-7; Hembry, pp.79-82.
4. Hembry, p.80; NA C11/2318/2; Centre for Kentish Studies Rusthall Manor MSS U749 M1; T. Rawlins, *Tunbridge Wells, or a Daie's Courtship: A Comedy* (1678); N. Luttrell, *Travels, 1670-1680 – Travel 13th to Tunbridge Wells*.
5. Lennard, pp.4, 5, 25. NA C11/320/1; CKS TR8 1671, 1673, 1680; CKS U749 T2.
7. CKS Weller–Poley MSS U38 T32.
8. CKSQ/SB22/4 NA C11/2318/2; C. Morris (ed.), *The Journeys of Celia Fiennes* (1947), p.133.
9. *Fiennes*, p.133; CKS U38 E1; Guildhall MS Sun Fire Register 24/388-9 1 Nov. 1727; J. Harris, *The History of Kent* (1719), p.292 (Engraving by Jan Kip): some of the features may be inaccurate, by comparison with the Map of 1738 (see 12 below).
10. Case of Baird v. the Corporation of Tunbridge Wells: Report on the Records in the Record Office; NA C11/386/4, C11/2318/2.
11. Ditto; *Abstract of Act, and Addenda for Confirming Certain Articles of Agreement made between the Lord of the Manor and the Freeholders* (Tunbridge Wells, 1881).
12. J. Bowra, *A Survey of Tunbridge Wells* (1738); Burr, p.101.
13. Harris, p.292 (Kip's engraving); *Abstract of Act …*
14. Burr, p.102.
15. NA C8/400/34, C110/154 (Part II).
16. CKS/U55 T385; Burr, p.106.
17. NA C6/100/7; R. Farthing, *A History of Mount Sion, Tunbridge Wells* (Chichester, 2003), pp.3, 10-11.
18. Farthing, pp.154-60, 441; Tonbridge Reference Library TU1 T57.
19. Farthing, pp.13, 32-3, 156.
20. NA C8/564/58; CKS U55 T429, T469, T473, T488.
21. NA C11/2318/2.
22. J.H. Thomas, 'Thomas Neale, a Seventeenth Century Projector', Southampton PhD thesis (1979), pp.xxiv, 151-4.
23. CKS U749, U38 E1; NA C5/222/22.
24. Farthing, pp.3-5, 38; NA C10/511/114.
25. CKS U749.
26. M. Barton, *Tunbridge Wells* (1987), p.88; Farthing, pp.109-11, 349-50.
27. NA C5/222/22; Farthing, p.112.
28. Fiennes, p.133.
29. Fiennes, p.133; CKS U55 T385.
30. Burr, p.106; A. Savidge, *Royal Tunbridge Wells* (Speldhurst, 1975), pp.50-1.
31. CKS DRb/Pi inventories of John Jeffery 21 April 1708 and William Latter 30 March 1728, both of Tonbridge; DRa/Pwr4 f.184, DRb/Pwr32 f.201, DRb/Pw55.
32. Savidge, pp.44-9; L.H. Waring, *The Story of the Church of King Charles the Martyr, Royal Tunbridge Wells* (Tunbridge Wells, 1937), p.5; J. Fuller, *A New History of King Charles the Martyr, Tunbridge Wells* (Tunbridge Wells, 2000), pp.1, 9, 14-22.
33. Savidge, p.49; Waring, pp.14-15.
34. CKS DRa/Pwr5 f.78; Farthing, pp.321, 442.
35. R. Farthing, *Royal Tunbridge Wells: A Pictorial History* (Chichester, 1990), picture 62.
36. T. Baker, *Tunbridge Walks, or the Yeoman of Kent: A Comedy* (1703), p.2; L. Melville, *Society at Tunbridge in the Eighteenth Century and After* (1912), pp.269-70.
37. Hembry, pp.233-4; Burr, pp.112-29; Melville pp.151-2.
38. Melville, pp.x, 212-53; Savidge, pp.72, 77, 88.
39. P. Amsinck, *Tunbridge Wells and its Neighbourhood* (1810), pp.16-17; Waring, pp.15-16; Melville, pp.121-3.
40. Savidge, pp.87-8.
41. CKS U749.
42. J. Sprange, *The Tunbridge Wells Guide* (Tunbridge Wells, 1780), p.88; J. Evans, *An Excursion to Brighton, a Visit to Tunbridge Wells* (Chiswick, 1821), p.153.
43. Sprange (1780), p.88.
44. Farthing, chapter 24.
45. CKS 'Estate of the Freehold Tenants of the Manor of Rusthall, recovered from the Lord of the Manor of Rusthall, 1770-1834' (1 volume of accounts).
46. CKS U746 and U749 A15, A17.
47. CKS U746 ; TRL TU1 E42/1.
48. Sprange (1780, 1801).
49. B. Austen, *Tunbridge Ware and Related European Decorative Woodwares* (1989), chapter 5; W. Finch, *Directory of Kent* (1803), pp.110-11; Waring, pp.15-16, 41-2; Fuller, p.45.
50. Savidge, pp.124-5; Melville, pp.274-83; P. Hembry (ed. and completed

by L.W. and E.E. Cowie), *British Spas from 1815 to the Present: a Social History* (1997), pp.3, 111.

51. CKS 'Estate of the Freehold Tenants ...'.

52. CKS U746 'New Baths – Abstract of Bills etc.'; U749 A15-20.

53. J. Phippen, *An Account of the Planting of the Royal Victoria Grove, at Tunbridge Wells* (Brighton, 1835).

54. C.W. Chalklin, 'Estate Development and the Beginnings of Modern Tunbridge Wells, 1800-40', *Archaeologia Cantiana* C 1984 (1985), p.389; Melville, p.263; *Clifford's Visitors Guide to Tunbridge Wells* (Tunbridge Wells, 1855), p.25.

55. National Archives Census Schedules 1841: HO107/463 (Tonbridge), HO107/462 (Speldhurst); Farthing, pp.285-91.

56. Chalklin, *Arch. Cant.*, pp.391-3, 395-6.

57. Ditto, pp.393-5; P. Whitbourn, *Decimus Burton Esquire Architect and Gentleman (1800-1881)*, Royal Tunbridge Wells Civic Society, Local History Monographs no.1, 2nd edn. (2006); Tunbridge Wells Museum: book of plans entitled 'The Calverley Estate in the Parish of Tonbridge and County of Kent, the property of John Ward Esq., 1829'.

58. *Clifford's Visitor Guide* (1855), p.25, Farthing, p.297; J. Clifford, *The Visitors Guide to Tunbridge Wells and its Environs* (1830), p.79; Savidge, p.209; H.R. Knipe (ed.), *Tunbridge Wells and Neighbourhood* (1916), p27; *Kent and Sussex Courier* 10 January 1992; Hembry, *British Spas from 1815*, pp.110-11.

59. Austen, pp.63-7.

60. H. Elwig, *Holy Trinity Church, Tunbridge Wells: A Centenary History* (1929), pp.6,7; Savidge, p.114.

61. Savidge, p.119.

62. *The Directory of the Ancient and Present State of Tunbridge Wells* (1816), pp.24, 42; J. Clifford, *The Tunbridge Wells Guide* (1817), p.329; J. Clifford, *A Descriptive Guide of Tunbridge Wells and its Environs* (1818), pp.15, 29, 30; Clifford, *The Visitor's Guide* (1830), pp.77-8.

63. Tunbridge Wells Borough Council: Tunbridge Wells Waterworks Company Minute Book, Vol. I; Savidge, p.122; Hembry, *British Spas from 1815*, p.106.

64. *Report of the Committee appointed to consider the question of a Local Act for Tunbridge Wells*, printed J. Clifford (Tunbridge Wells, 1832); Hembry, *British Spas from 1815*, p.107.

65. TWBC Local Act Committee Minute Book, Vol.I (1833-34).

66. *An Act for Lighting, Watching, Cleansing, Regulating and Improving the Town of Tunbridge Wells* (1835).

Part Two: The Growth of the Modern Town

1. *Maidstone Journal*, 21 June 1831; Savidge, pp.128-31; B.R. Mitchell and P. Deane, *Abstract of British Historical Statistics* (Cambridge, 1962), pp.5, 8-9.

2. NA HO107/462 and HO107/463/1-20.

3. R.S. Neale, *Bath: A Social History 1680-1850* (1981), p.276.

4. NA Census 1871 (RG12) Speldhurst.

5. Farthing, chapter 20; S. Brown and A. Bates, 'Woodbury Park Road, Park Road and GrosvenorPark', in J. Cunningham (ed.), *The Residential Parks of Tunbridge Wells*, RTW Civic Society Local History no,4 (2004), p.49; Savidge p.135.

6. This paragraph and the three preceding ones are based on Savidge, p.135, and P. Whitbourn, 'Calverley Park', G. and B. Copus, 'Nevill Park and Hungershall Park', 'Camden Park' and 'Bishops Down Park, Molyneux Park and Boyne Park', S. Brown and A. Bates, op.cit., A. Bates and J. Cunningham, 'The Changing Concept and the Changing Town: St James' Park and Ferndale Park, Sherwood Park, Sandown Park and Sandhurst Park', in J. Cunningham (ed.), pp.12-61; Kent Historic Buildings Committee, *The Kent Historic Buildings Index: Tunbridge Wells Section* no.1 (1999), pp.74-85.

7. Savidge, pp.135, 139, 155; G. Stevens, *Directory of Tunbridge Wells, Tonbridge and Neighbourhood* (1886), p.26 etc.; *Kent and Sussex Courier* 21 August 1992.

8. R. Homan, *The Victorian Churches of Kent* (Chichester, 1984), pp.96-8.

9. Savidge, p.132; Brown and Bates, p.49, Bates and Cunningham, p.55; Tunbridge Wells Reference Library: House History (file) section 4 St Johns North and East: S. Brown, 'The Early History of Upper Grosvenor Road'.

10. M. Roake (ed.), *Religious Worship in Kent: the Census of 1851*, Kent Records (Maidstone, 1999), pp.143-6; N. Yates, 'The Major Kent Towns in the religious Census of 1851', *Arch. Cant.* C, pp.399-423.

11. Savidge, p.150; W.N. Yates, 'Bells and Smells: Brighton and South Coast Religion Reconsidered', *Southern History* 5 (1983), pp.139-40; Homan, pp.97-8.

12. J.H. Townsend, *Edward Hoare MA. A Record of his Life* (1896); Savidge, pp.146-7, 157-8.

13. Savidge, pp.43, 55-8.

14. Stevens, pp.43-50, 55-8.

15. Stevens, pp.26-30, 44-6, 50, 58-9; Savidge, pp.151, 155, 159.

16. T.W.B.C. Local Act minute book no.1 (1835-38) ff.1-52, Police Committee minute book 1835-39; W. Brackett, *Rides and Drives in the Neighbourhood of Tunbridge Wells* (Tunbridge Wells, 1858), p.118; *Brackett's Descriptive Illustrated Hand Guide to Tunbridge Wells* (1863),

p.129; *Tunbridge Wells Gazette* 6 January 1860; *Mathieson's Tunbridge Wells and Tunbridge Directory for 1867-68* (Tunbridge Wells, 1868), p.114.

17. TWBC Police Committee minute book 1835-39, Local Government Act minute book no.1 f.23; *Stapley's Tunbridge Wells Visitor's Guide* (Tunbridge Wells, 1847), pp.48-9; Stevens, pp.35-6, 49.

18. Savidge, pp.159-60; Stevens, pp.20-2; *Tunbridge Wells Gazette* 6 January 1860; TWBC Local Act Committee minute book vol.II (1834-35) 11 May 1835, Local Act minute book no.1 f.24, Police Committee minute book 1835-39: 21 August 1835.

19. Farthing, chapter 27; Savidge, p.160.

20. *Kelly's Directory of Tunbridge Wells* (1934), pp.A16-18; Savidge, pp.160-2, 166; C.H. Strange, 'The History of Tunbridge Wells', in J.C.M. Given (ed.), *Royal Tunbridge Wells Past and Present* (Tunbridge Wells, 1946), pp.48-9; *Kent and Sussex Courier* 19 June 1992.

21. G. and B. Copus, 'Bishops Down Park ...', pp.33-43, A. Bates and J. Cunningham, 'The Changing Concept ...', pp.52-62, and 'Linden Park, Madeira Park and Warwick Park', pp.63-71, in Cunningham (ed.), *The Residential Parks ...*; *Kelly's Directory of Tunbridge Wells* (1909).

22. Strange, pp.49-51, 54-5; Savidge, pp. 171-2, 175, 179-80.

23. Homan, pp.97-8; *Kelly's Directory ...* (1934), p.A17, 465.

24. H.R. Knipe, *Tunbridge Wells and Neighbourhood* (Tunbridge Wells, 1916), pp.33-5; Strange, p.53; Savidge, pp.166-70, 172, 175-6, 179-80; *Kelly's Directory ...* (1909), p.203.

25. *Kelly's Directory ...* (1909) *passim*; J. Butcher, *Tunbridge Wells: I was Born on the Pantiles* (Tunbridge Wells 1990), pp.1-3, 8-9, 50.

26. Savidge, pp.172-5; Strange, pp.51-2.

27. *Kelly's Directory ...* (1909); *Kent and Sussex Courier* 23 November 2007; Savidge, pp.177-9; M. Tapsell, *Memories of Kent Cinemas* (Croydon, 1987), p.97; G. Smith, *Concise History of English Carriages Past and Present* (Tunbridge Wells, 1896), pp.55, 95.

28. *Kelly's Directory ...* (1909); Strange, pp.60-1; lecture by Dr A. Logan to Tonbridge Historical Society November 2007.

29. Savidge, pp.168-70, 179-80.

30. Savidge, pp.167-8; Farthing, *Mount Sion*, pp.114-15, 316-17; Strange, pp.48-9; H. Elwig, *A Biographical Dictionary of Notable People at Tunbridge Wells* (1941), pp. 18-19.

31. Strange, pp.56-7; Savidge, p.183; [A. Scott] *Some War Work in Tunbridge Wells May 1915 – April 1919* (Tunbridge Wells, 1919).

32. R. Farthing, *Royal Tunbridge Wells: A Pictorial History* (1990), 'Introduction'; *Census of England and Wales, 1911*, ditto, 1931; *Kelly's Directory ...* (1934), ditto (1940); Cunningham 'Great Culverden Park', in Cunningham (ed.), *Residential Parks*, pp.72-9.

33. *Sixty Years of Service: The Kent and Sussex Hospital, a History* (Tunbridge Wells, 1988), pp.10-18; John Jarvis Ltd, *Souvenir of the New Kent and Sussex Hospital, Mount Ephraim, Tunbridge Wells* (1934), p.32.

34. J. Cunningham (ed.), for Members of the Local History Group of the Royal Tunbridge Wells Civic Society, *Four Hundred Years of the Wells*, Civic Society Monograph no.5 (2005), p.141; Strange, pp.62-3; *The Builder* 16 November 1934.

35. *Kelly's Directory ...* (1934), pp.A20-1; Strange, pp.58-9.

36. *Kelly's Directory ...* (1934); Austen, pp.120-9.

37. R. Cobb, *Still Life and Sketches from a Tunbridge Wells Childhood* (1983), p.74; *Kelly's Directory ...* (1934).

38. *Kelly's Directory ...* (1934); Strange, p.56; *Kent and Sussex Courier* 5 January, 2 February and 7 December 1934; *Kent and Sussex Courier* 6 December 1991.

39. Strange, pp.60-1.

40. Strange, pp.61-2; Tapsell, pp.97-9; *Kent and Sussex Courier* 2 and 23 February 1934.

41. *Kelly's Directory ...* (1934); Strange, p.60.

42. *Kent and Sussex Courier* 5 January and 2 February 1934.

43. I. Beavis, 'Fighting for the Future' in Cunningham (ed.), *Four Hundred Years*, pp.124-42.

44. Elwig, pp.19, 40; Savidge, p.164; *Kent and Sussex Courier* 2 February 1934; Cobb, pp.70, 141-2; family information about A.N. Edwards.

45. A. Bates, 'The Second World War and its Aftermath 1939-1953' in Cunningham (ed.), *Four Hundred Years*, pp.143-62; [F.C. Squirrell] *Civil Defence: a History of Civil Defence in the Borough of Tunbridge Wells 1939-45*, pp.4, 29, 38; A. Noble, *Tunbridge Wells: a History and Celebration* (2004), pp.88-93.

46. N. Yates (ed.), *Kent in the Twentieth Century* (Woodbridge, 2001), p.14.

47. Bates, pp.162-8; Noble, pp.93-4.

48. *Royal Tunbridge Wells* (Tunbridge Wells, [1955]) [an Official Guide].

49. *Kelly's Directory of Tunbridge Wells* (1950); Bates, pp.167-8.

50. Savidge, p.195.

51. Savidge, pp.184-7; *Kelly's Directory of Tunbridge Wells* (1963), ditto (1974); *Kent and Sussex Courier* 11 September 1992; *The Story of Caffyns from 1865*, p.27.

52. *Kelly's Directory ...* (1963), ditto (1974).

53. *Education in Kent, 1948-1953, 1953 – 1958, 1958 – 1963, 1963 – 1968, 1968 – 1974* (Kent Education Committee, Maidstone).

54. *Sixty Years of Service*, pp.20-1, 34-7.

Sources

References are given in full in the Notes. Important secondary sources are mentioned in the Acknowledgements and the Introduction. S. Brown (compiled), *Researching Royal Tunbridge Wells: a Bibliography of Historical Sources*, Royal Tunbridge Wells Civic Society Local History Monograph no.2 (2003) is a catalogue of the printed material in the Tunbridge Wells Reference Library.

The long series of guide books and directories, printed on behalf of the visitors, is exceptional. They were published every two or three years, beginning with R. Oneley, *A General Account of Tunbridge Wells and its Environs* (1771) and J. Sprange, *The Tunbridge Wells Guide* (1780), and ending with *Kelly's Directory of Tunbridge Wells* (1974). Kent directories with sections on Tunbridge Wells are also useful. Especially helpful are their lists of inhabitants with occupations; for assistant tradesmen and craftsmen, clerks and labourers one needs to refer to the decennial MS census available in the National Archives with copies in the Tunbridge Wells Library. T.B. Burr, *A History of Tunbridge Wells* (1766) has mistakes in the 17th-century account, though its later survey is helpful.

Newspapers include *The Visitor* (1833-5), *Sussex Agricultural Express* (1837-52), *Tunbridge Wells Gazette* (1855-93), *Tunbridge Wells Journal* (1862-1904) and *Kent and Sussex Courier* (from 1873). They are available on microfilm in the Tunbridge Wells Library. The *Maidstone Journal* from the 1780s covers Tunbridge Wells, the earlier part being available on microfilm in Tonbridge as well as Maidstone Libraries.

Important among the recent writings of the Civic Society Local History Group are the contributions of Philip Whitbourn on Decimus Burton and Beulah Road, John Cunningham's edition of *The Residential Parks of Tunbridge Wells* (2004) and of *Four Hundred Years of the Wells* (2005). There is also A. Noble, *Tunbridge Wells: a History and Celebration* (2004). The latest history of King Charles Chapel (more recently Church) is by J. Fuller (2000).

In the Museum are the minutes of the Local Board, 1835-89, and of the Borough Council from 1889, with minutes of their committees. The newspapers contain reports of their meetings.

The National Archives hold the MS Chancery Proceedings, being the statements of the parties in the lawsuits, with depositions of witnesses; they thus include much contemporary comment. The Centre of Kentish Studies hold family and estate MSS, including title deeds, accounts, business papers and correspondence. All these records are the basis of the 17th- and 18th-century history.

The numbered illustrations come from the following:

T. Davis, *Tunbridge Wells: the Gentle Aspect* (Chichester, 1976), p.58: Part One opening page; p.59: Part Two opening page; p.19: no.50; p.58: no.51.

British Library: Add. MS 5233 folio 72: no.1; Maps 3110 (29): nos. 8, 9, 14. Copyright: British Library Board, all rights reserved.

M. Barton, *Tunbridge Wells* (1937), p.108: no.2; p.180: no.4; p.236: no.6.

Postcards, with date when postmarked and name of publisher when stated, are Common 1907: no.3; Mount Ephraim and Common *c.*1905: no.5; Grove, Mount Sion 1905: no.16; King Charles Church 1906 published H.G. Groves, the Pantiles: no.19; High Rocks *c.*1905: no.22; Toad Rock 1943, published Photochrom Co. Ltd: no.23; Mount Ephraim mansion *c.*1905: no.34; Common and Mount Ephraim 1912, published Valentine's X.L. Series: no.36; Common with townspeople 1906, published Photochrom Co. Ltd: no.42; Christ Church: no.54; St Mark, Broadwater Down, published Photochrom Co. Ltd: no.55; St James 1906: no.56; St Peter, published Photochrom Co. Ltd: no.57; St Barnabas 1912, published Photochrom Co. Ltd: no.58; Opera House 1904: no.66; General Post Office 1908, published W.J. Walter Picture Frame Maker, Holly Bush, Crescent Road: no.67; General Hospital, Grosvenor Road *c.*1905-10, published H. Jenkins [photographer 20 Grosvenor Road]: no.68; St John 1904: no.70; Grosvenor Recreation Ground 1911, published Valentines Series: no.71; Mount Pleasant and Central Station, published Valentines Series: no.72; Calverley Road 1907, published Valentines Series: no.73; Pantiles 1906, published Valentines Series: no.74; Mount Pleasant 1905, published by H.G. Groves, The Pantiles: no.76; Opera House and Calverley Parade 1908, published Giesen and Co, London E.C: no.77; High Street 1906, published Valentines Series: no.78; Frant Road 1916: no.79; Commercial Hotel 1912-13: no.80; London Road and Vale Royal pre-1918, published Boots Cash Chemists 'Pelham' Series: no.81; Cumberland Villa 1906: no.82; War Memorial post-1923: no.84; Top of Mount Pleasant post-1923, published Photogravure Series: no.85; Water Dippers at Well 1925, published North Hants Printing Co., Fleet: no.86; Civic Centre in 1950s: no.87; Lower High Street in 1930s, published Photochrom Co. Ltd: no.88; Church Road 1955, published Percy G. Pratt [141 Camden Road]: no.91; Calverley Road in 1950s: no.92. These postcards belong to the author.

R. Farthing, *A History of Mount Sion, Tunbridge Wells* (Chichester, 2003), p.16 'Brooke/Constable Partition 1686', Kent Archaeological Society Ward Collection Tonbridge File: no.7; p.154 'Queen Anne's Mansion or Sion Crescent – Camburn postcard – about 1910': no.12; p.8 'Martins Lower House – rear view (now nos 59-61 High Street)': no.15.

R. Farthing, *Royal Tunbridge Wells: a Pictorial History* (Chichester, 1990), illustration 29: no.10; illustration 64: no.26; illustration 82: no.41; illustration 58: no.46.

Photographs taken April 2008: nos.11, 13, 17, 32, 33, 38, 39, 48, 49, 52, 53, 59, 60, 62-5, 69, 89, 90, 93.

Kent and Sussex Courier 12 June 1992: no.40; 19 June 1992: no.61; 26 June 1992: no.75; 11 September 1992: no.83.

L. Melville, *Society at Royal Tunbridge Wells in the Eighteenth Century and After* (1912), p.52: no.18; p.128: no.20; p.80: no.21; p.94: no.24; p.326: no.25; p.66: no.27; p.272: no.28; p.218: no.29; p.278: no.30; p.262: no.31.

J. Britton, *Descriptive Sketches of Tunbridge Wells and the Calverley Estate* (1832), facing title: no.35; p.54: no.37; p.56: no.44; p.56: no.45.

Index